WHEN LIFE KNOCKS YOU DOWN, COME BACK STRONGER

How I Went from Federal Inmate to Owner of a Multi-million Dollar Law Practice in 5 Years

JIMMY FASIG

WITH ACTIVITIES BY
AUDRA FOURNIER

CONTENTS

Introduction 5

Chapter 1:   The Magic of Goal Setting and the Power of the Subconscious Mind 7

Chapter 2:   But Seriously, How Did I Do It?. 13

Chapter 3:   The Reticular Activating System. 18

Chapter 4:   Overcome the Fear of Failure. 23

Chapter 5:   The Power of Beliefs 34

Chapter 6:   Claim Your Power 40

Chapter 7:   The Power of Why 46

Chapter 8:   How Do You Discover Your Mission in Life?. 51

Chapter 9:   Create a Mission Statement 59

Chapter 10: Deconstructing Dreams and Visions . . 62

Chapter 11: Putting the Pieces Together 71

Chapter 12: The Global Consciousness Project . . . 79

Chapter 13: Embrace the Reality of Infinite Possible Futures. 84

Chapter 14:	Create Big, Bold, Amazing Goals	91
Chapter 15:	Create a Master Goal	99
Chapter 16:	Become the Person You Must to Achieve Your Goal	102
Chapter 17:	Identify What's Holding You Back	114
Chapter 18:	Identify Negative Beliefs and Turn Them Upside Down	124
Chapter 19:	Unity Consciousness: The Ultimate Empowering Belief	129
Chapter 20:	Living in the Flow	141
Chapter 21:	Some Final Thoughts	145

INTRODUCTION

Life comes down to a series of moments. Some are painful; others are joyful. The ironic truth is that our most painful moments are often the catalysts for our most immense experiences of joy. The greater the pain we endure, the greater our capacity for joy becomes. When we find meaning and purpose behind our suffering, we can finally transcend our suffering and experience levels of joy we never knew existed.

My name is Jimmy Fasig, and this is a true story about how I turned my greatest challenge into my biggest opportunity. I used to be a drug dealer. Now, I'm a lawyer. I spent two-and-a-half years in prison, where I learned how it feels to be scared and powerless. I'm five-foot-five and weighed 135 pounds when I turned myself in to the federal detention center. I was threatened with violence on numerous occasions. One inmate threatened me with a broomstick, another with a lock. I had to challenge a muscle-bound tough guy to a fight because he wouldn't stop harassing me. I experienced strip searches and solitary confinement. I was afraid I would never get a good job after my release; I thought no woman would ever love me. I never wanted to feel that way again, so I made plans to reclaim my power.

Most people would have predicted that with a felony conviction I could never become a lawyer. As I sit here writing this book, I am the managing partner of a multimillion-dollar law firm with offices across Florida. I am currently living a life I could barely dare to dream while in prison. The purpose of this book is to share the lessons that allowed me to rise from prison to paradise and to provide people everywhere with the tools they need to overcome obstacles and come back stronger.

A warning from the beginning: this book goes deep. It's not your every-day self-help book. Success isn't a one-size-fits-all subject, so what works for one person might not work for someone else. But it's always the inner work that ultimately leads to positive outcomes in a person's life. You can't achieve lasting, enduring success without working on yourself: that's without a doubt our biggest challenge, and it's often our greatest fear.

The circumstances we experience in life are a direct reflection of who we are. In order to experience a different life, we have to become a different person. The lessons in this book will guide you to becoming your greatest self, a master of self, which in turn will allow you to live your greatest life.

CHAPTER 1

THE MAGIC OF GOAL SETTING AND THE POWER OF THE SUBCONSCIOUS MIND

How did I go from prisoner to law partner within five years of my release from prison? Short answer: I was a consummate goal setter. There seems to be something magical about setting goals, writing them down, and making plans to accomplish them. When you write down a goal, your subconscious mind goes to work figuring out the best and most efficient way to achieve it. The results can be amazing because the subconscious mind is much more aware and powerful than the conscious mind. I'm going to share with you a personal story about how goal setting worked for me, and we'll spend much of this book unpacking the lessons contained within the story.

During my 2 ½ year stint in prison, I spent most of my time reading self-help books, trying to prepare myself for my release. I created a five-year plan for what my life would look like once I got out. I was released to a halfway house in December of 1999. In my five-year plan, I wrote that by December 31, 2005, I would be a lawyer, the partner of a law firm, and that I would own my own house, have perfect credit, and own a silver Mercedes SL 500 convertible. I ripped a picture of the Mercedes out of a magazine and taped it to my prison locker. I wrote my goals down over and over and psyched myself up into a highly emotional state as I visualized myself achieving these goals every day.

Keep in mind, I was a convicted felon who was just about to be released from prison. I had been arrested for drug trafficking while I was in law school. The idea of becoming a lawyer—much less the partner of a law firm—within five years after my release was extremely ambitious, to say the least. Nevertheless, in September of 2005, three months before the five-year deadline, I was accepted to the Florida Bar unconditionally. I was officially a lawyer! That very same week, I was offered a partnership at the well-established law firm where I had been working as a paralegal since my prison release. I had perfect credit and had purchased not only one house, but three. The only goal I had written down that I didn't achieve was buying that silver Mercedes SL 500 convertible. I had put the Mercedes out of my mind, because I had decided to invest my money in real estate. I had no idea that the universe had heard my call and was going to grant me that Mercedes anyway, whether I pursued it or not.

Fast forward three months later to December of 2005, the very month that I had set as the deadline for achieving my Mercedes goal. It was the holidays, so my stepfather had called me and invited me to a Christmas party. I was hesitant to go, because the party was almost two hours away from where I lived. I hadn't seen my Mom and stepdad for a while, so I felt compelled to accept the invitation. When I arrived, I found out that it was a Mercedes Club party—I hadn't even realized that my stepdad was part of a Mercedes Club. Except for my wife (fiancé at the time) and me, everybody in the room was at least 60 years old. I had just turned 35, and my wife was 24. I remember saying to my wife, "What are we doing here?" To start the party off, a white-haired lady stood up and asked the room which of us had driven the furthest to get there. I raised my hand and explained that I had driven from Tallahassee to Defuniak Springs. She responded, "Congratulations, you just won a silver Mercedes SL 500 convertible!" She showed me the car. It was the same make, same model, same color, and had the same body style as the picture of the car I had posted on my prison locker! The only catch: It was the Matchbox version, big enough to fit in the palm of my hand.

Some people might choose to see this as a coincidence, but the chances of it happening randomly—with the same make, model, color, and body style right before my December 31st deadline—are so astronomical it boggles the mind. The size of the car doesn't matter. What matters is what this says about the power of the subconscious mind and its ability to direct us toward our goals. My subconscious mind gave me exactly what I had instructed when I wrote down repeatedly, "I own a silver, convertible, Mercedes SL500 by December 31, 2005." There is no directly identifiable cause and effect relationship between the goal and the way it was realized. I had no plans or intention to go to a Mercedes Club Christmas party—I just so happened to be the person at the party who had driven the furthest to get there. They didn't give away any other prizes. It seemed like a completely random choice to give out that particular make, model, and color Mercedes.

One obvious conclusion I gathered from the Mercedes experience is that it's important to visualize yourself experiencing the goal as already accomplished. I should have visualized myself inside of the Mercedes with the top down and the wind blowing through my hair. If I had done that, I might have gotten a full-sized car. The more important lesson, however, is this: the human mind is unbelievably powerful. When we set a goal with emotion and passion, it will lead us exactly where we want to go. We don't have to know how we'll achieve the goal. We just have to believe the goal is achievable, visualize ourselves achieving it (with emotion), trust our subconscious mind to direct us toward the most efficient path to our goal, and finally, move in the direction we feel guided to pursue while maintaining our focus on the goal. Maintaining focus on the goal is the key, because the dominant thoughts that occupy our minds determine the reality we experience.

 Activity:

What are the dominant thoughts that occupy your mind? In other words, what do you think about most often?

_____
_____
_____
_____
_____
_____

How have those thoughts contributed to manifesting your current circumstances?

_____
_____
_____
_____
_____
_____

How would your life be different if your dominant thoughts over the last five years had been focused on reaching your goals?

_____
_____
_____
_____
_____

How could your life be different five years from now if your dominant thoughts became focused on achieving your highest goals?

_____
_____
_____
_____
_____

CHAPTER 2

But Seriously, How Did I Do It?

The Mercedes story shows that setting goals can produce what appear to be magical results, but in reality, there is nothing magical about it. In the pages to come, we'll spend some time discussing the nuts and bolts of how the Mercedes manifested in my life, but the most immediate question is, "How did I become a lawyer and partner of a law firm in five short years after my release from prison?" Other than setting it as a goal, what other factors came into play in determining my success or failure?

The first factor is that I believed becoming a partner in a law firm was possible, so I made it an all-consuming obsession. My entire drug dealing career happened while I was in law school. Fortunately, I was smart enough not to sell drugs on campus, which saved me from getting expelled from school. After getting arrested, I approached the law school dean and told her about my arrest. She shared with me a story about a man who had been convicted of selling marijuana but later became a lawyer. She told me this lawyer had joined an organization called Florida Lawyers Assistance, which is an organization dedicated to helping law students and lawyers who develop drug and alcohol issues. With the help of this organization, he was able to convince the Florida Bar that he had been rehabilitated, and after getting his civil rights restored and passing the Bar exam, he was given a license to practice law. If somebody else can do it, I reasoned, there's no reason I couldn't. All I needed to know was that it was possible. I practically burned my fingers on the phone keys dialing so fast to Florida Lawyers Assistance.

Like most people who get involved in dealing drugs, part of my problem was a drug and alcohol habit I had developed during law school. During spring break of my second year of law school, I traveled to Amsterdam to meet my girlfriend at the time who was studying abroad in Germany. While there, I tried the drug ecstasy for the first time, and I quickly became obsessed with chasing the high I felt on ecstasy. That led to me trying other drugs and developing a habit, and ultimately becoming a drug dealer to support my habit. Fortunately, the Florida Bar considers drug and alcohol addiction a condition that can be rehabilitated. The Florida Lawyers Assistance program set out a road map for me to prove to the Bar that I had been rehabilitated. Nothing was going to stop me from doing exactly what they said I should do, which brings us to the second factor that makes a difference between success and failure- a burning desire. Our desire to achieve the goal must be strong enough to overcome the fear of failure, self doubt, laziness, and everything else that might hold us back. We have to want it so bad that we are willing to change who we are at our core.

My desire to become a partner in a law firm was so strong I was determined to do whatever it took. I knew that to become a law partner, I had to become an entirely different person. I had to become the type of person who would be a partner in a law firm. I had been sentenced to five years in prison, but I was released after two-and-a-half years because I submitted to a drug and alcohol rehabilitation program. After my release from prison, I voluntarily attended Alcoholics and Narcotics Anonymous meetings, and I submitted to random urine tests so that I could prove that I was free from drugs and alcohol in my system. I kept records of every meeting I went to, and I called into a call center every day to see if my number came up for a random urine test. I also connected with a sponsor, another person in the Alcoholics Anonymous program who could testify on my behalf about my rehabilitation efforts.

Meanwhile, when I got out of prison, I got a job as a paralegal making $10.00 per hour in an established law firm. Remember, my goal was not only to become a lawyer, but to become a partner in a law firm. I worked as hard a human being could possibly work at that job, and the partners in the firm began to take notice. My pay quickly increased to $15.00 per hour, and I was given the opportunity to work as much overtime as I wanted.

I was a focused, goal setting machine, working 70 to 80 hours a week or more. I knew that to prove my value to the firm I had to show the partners the results I was producing. In the personal injury business, results are measured by settlements. I calculated the amount of settlements I needed to produce so that the firm was profitable, and I set the goal of producing more than that. I broke my goals down to yearly, monthly, weekly, and even daily goals, and I worked from my goals list every single day. For my long-term goals, I wrote out a contract, promising myself that I would reach those goals. My wife framed the contract, and I put it beside my bed to review every morning when I awoke and every night before I went to bed.

I also knew that to become a partner in the firm I had to make myself indispensable, so I took as much responsibility off of the two senior partners as possible. I created a document-merging computer program that allowed me to work much more efficiently than the other paralegals. As a result, I was producing greater and faster results on cases where the senior partners had to do less work. The other paralegals started complaining that I must be cutting corners, because in their minds no human being could produce at the level I was producing without cheating. That's when a golden opportunity arose for me.

CHAPTER 3

THE RETICULAR ACTIVATING SYSTEM

The thing about setting a goal is that the act of setting the goal opens your mind to opportunities that you might not otherwise have noticed. The subconscious mind takes in all of the information around it, which is then filtered by the brain, which sifts out all of the information that isn't relevant to our survival, safety, and wants. Because the information is being filtered, we only become consciously aware of a tiny fraction of the information that is available to us—if we were consciously aware of all of it, we'd be overwhelmed. This filtering function has been labeled the brain's reticular activating system.

The reticular activating system directs the individual's attention to anything in their environment that pertains to the satisfaction of that individual's desires. When someone has conflicting or unclear desires, the reticular activating system directs their attention in a scattered way. However, when a person has clear goals with a clear mission, the reticular activating system goes to work, seeking the most efficient possible way to achieve the goals. The goal-setter starts to have ideas and notice opportunities for reaching the goal: the opportunities were always there; they just never noticed them. The results of goalsetting can seem like magic, but they are really just the result of opening your mind to the possibility of achieving a goal and letting the subconscious mind direct you to where you want to go.

When the other paralegals in my law firm started to complain about my productivity being too high, I noticed an opportunity. The senior partner at the time called a paralegal meeting, where he berated all of us, including me, for the firm's overall lack of productivity. The verbal lashing was so bad, a lot of people in my position would have been disheartened, but I knew his wrath should not have been directed at me personally. I was producing results whereas the other paralegals weren't. Because I had a goal of becoming a partner in the firm, I took it as an opportunity to show my value and make myself indispensable. After the meeting, I went to the senior partner's office and told him I had a solution to the firm's productivity problem. I showed him the numbers that proved my productivity, and he could clearly see that I was producing results.

"Make me head paralegal," I said. "Put me in charge of all of the other paralegals, and I'll guarantee at least five settlement demands per week." Settlement demands are letters we send to insurance companies to initiate settlement negotiations on personal injury cases. The demand letters are how we make money, in most cases. In exchange for the guarantee of five demand letters per week, I asked for a raise to $22.22 per hour and permission to work as much overtime as I wanted.

The senior partner gave me exactly what I wanted. I worked day and night, sometimes showing up to work at 3:30 A.M. and leaving after midnight. Not only did I deliver on my promise to produce five demand letters per week, I made both of the senior partners' jobs so easy they didn't even have to show up for work most days if they didn't want to. They're good lawyers, so they stayed involved, but I made sure they felt confident I had their caseloads under control. I met with clients, negotiated settlements, and handled most cases from inception to conclusion, bothering the senior partners as little as possible. The Florida Bar rules require a lawyer to direct and control settlement negotiations and advise clients, so we all made sure to follow the rules, but I served as their liaison for it all. I let the partners know that I was expecting to be offered a partnership when I became a member of the Bar.

The increased pay allowed me to pay off all my debts and hire a lawyer for $7,500 to help me get my civil rights restored. That allowed me to take the Bar exam. I then hired another lawyer for $5,000 to represent me in front of the Board of Bar Examiners, to prove I'd been rehabilitated. By that time, I had been working at the same job as a paralegal for almost five years, had perfect credit, had purchased three houses, and had glowing recommendations from the senior partners of my firm. When I testified in front of the Board of Bar Examiners, I shared with them my obsession with reading self-help books and goal setting. I shared with them my goal of becoming partner in the firm. On September 5, 2005, I received a letter from the Board of Bar Examiners. "You have been accepted into the Florida Bar unconditionally."

That very week, one of the senior partners came into my office and offered me a partnership. He offered to give me 10% of the firm, free of charge. My goal was coming to fruition! Believe it or not, I was so brazen at the time, and so overly confident due to my own mental programming, I turned down the offer and demanded 20%. As I look back on it today, I have a hard time believing this- they gave me 10% of the firm and sold me another 10%, making me 20% owner of a well-established law firm as soon as I became a member of the Bar! Most lawyers expect to work seven years as an associate lawyer in a firm before even being considered for partnership.

There are so many lessons packed into this story, it will take some time to unravel them all. The remainder of this book will offer insights into how and why the goalsetting worked for me, so that the reader can implement those lessons and apply them to his or her own life. I'll also share with you other personal stories that illustrate important lessons I learned along the way. Finally, I'll share with you what I consider to be the ultimate empowering belief, which supercharges our ability to set and achieve amazing goals in the shortest time possible.

CHAPTER 4

OVERCOME THE FEAR OF FAILURE

Most people are afraid to set goals because they are afraid to fail: it's the number-one reason people choose not to pursue the future that they desire. They're afraid that if they try and fail, they will feel even worse about themselves than they already do. The reality is that the most successful people in the world are also the biggest failures. Failure is the key to success.

Abraham Lincoln, for example, is widely regarded as one of the greatest presidents that ever lived; he succeeded in abolishing slavery. But what most people don't know is that Abraham Lincoln was a huge failure before he succeeded. As a young man, he worked as a store clerk and a boatman to support his family. While still a teenager, he built a flatboat, which he used to transport produce down the Mississippi River, but he ended up having to sell the flatboat for its timber. That was his first business failure. Lincoln then built another flatboat and worked as an independent operator, but his business failed again in 1831. In 1832, he ran for the Illinois state legislature and lost, then started a general store with a partner. That business also failed and left him with a huge debt. In 1834, he ran for the state legislature again and won, but the next year his fiancé died and left him heartbroken, and he later had a nervous breakdown and spent six months in bed. In 1838, he sought to become the speaker of the state legislature and was defeated; he then sought to become an elector, was defeated, ran for congress, and was defeated again. He lost his bid for re-election in 1848. He ran for the senate in 1854 and lost. In 1856, he sought the vice presidential nomination and got less than 100 votes; two years later, he ran for the Senate again and lost. Finally, in 1860, he was elected President of the United States.

If Abraham Lincoln had succumbed to the fear of failure, who knows what type of world we would be living in today. Instead, he moved forward with boldness and persistence, and he became one of the greatest historical figures of all time. No matter how many times he failed, he never gave up. For Abraham Lincoln, his mission was bigger than whatever fear he had of failure. For Abraham, failure was not an option.

Embrace the Power of Failure

Most people fear failure, because they don't understand it's power. Failure is the subconscious mind's way of helping us get what we truly want—it can be a way of encouraging us to change our trajectory, so that we can move onto something greater and more fulfilling. At other times, the subconscious mind uses failure as a way of teaching us lessons, so we can try again with a greater chance of success. For me, my failures have been a critical part of my successes. My experience as a drug dealer gave me amazing insight into how the subconscious mind uses failure as a tool to direct us to the future reality we truly want, as opposed to the one we think we want.

When I first started law school in 1992, I had no idea what I truly wanted. I wanted to be a lawyer because they made lots of money, dated pretty girls, and wore cool suits. I didn't care about other people, except to the extent that they could help me get what I wanted. I was on a trajectory for becoming a corporate lawyer who worked eighty hours a week and worshipped money.

The night I took the first ecstasy pill in Amsterdam, I had no idea how it would change my life. At the time, I was extremely judgmental, and I thought people who did drugs were losers. But we were in Amsterdam. I hadn't seen my then-girlfriend for months, and it was awkward. A French guy sat at our table at the night club and asked if we wanted to try ecstasy. I could see on my girlfriend's face that she wanted to try it, so we broke an ecstasy pill in half and shared it.

About fifteen minutes after I took that pill, I started to transform. That night was the most incredible experience I had ever had, at least up until that period in my life. For the first time, I felt connected to the world and to everyone else in the world. The high from the ecstasy wiped away my fear and judgment of other people, so that by the end of the night, I had a new group of friends. My girlfriend and I were supposed to travel to Germany the next day, but we were having so much fun, we stayed in Amsterdam the entire week of spring break, getting high on ecstasy most of the time.

When I arrived back in the United States, I no longer cared about law school. I had no interest in being a lawyer. All I wanted was to chase the high I had experienced in Amsterdam. The only reason I finished my second year of law school was because of the momentum I had already created going into spring break. That summer, I worked as a judicial clerk in Orlando and spent most of my free time trying to find good ecstasy pills, which was not an easy task. By the end of it, I had experimented with LSD, cocaine, and magic mushrooms. I was completely lost.

When my third and final year of law school arrived, I didn't even bother registering for classes. I started selling grams and eight balls of cocaine, making enough money to survive, chase women, and pursue my interest in finding good ecstasy pills. Before long, I saw an opportunity to sell cocaine in larger amounts. I went down to Miami with barely enough money to get back to Tallahassee, which was where I was supposed to be studying, and by the time I left, I had found a connection who fronted me a quarter kilo of cocaine for $6,250. I sold that quarter kilo in less than a week and doubled my money.

Fast forward to the summer before my fourth year of law school. Law school is supposed to be a three-year endeavor, but Florida State University allows students to take up to four years to complete the curriculum. By this time, I had no plans to go back to law school. I was selling a kilo of cocaine every week, making about $10,000 on every kilo I sold, but I was spending the money as fast as I was making it. I had an entourage of drug users who followed me everywhere. We ate at steak houses and sushi restaurants twice a day. Most days, we woke up around noon, met at a Roadhouse Grill, ate and drank liquor for lunch, and started doing cocaine at around 2:00 P.M. We went to clubs every night and took ecstasy every time we had the chance. I paid for everything with the drug money.

The end of that summer was a major turning point for me. Another drug dealer invited me to go to with him to Cancun for vacation. We rented a hotel room on the beach, and we partied as hard as I've ever partied. One morning, I woke up after a long night and walked out to the balcony of the hotel, which looked out over the Mexican beach. Hundreds of suntanned people were enjoying their vacations. It was a beautiful, sunny day, and the beach was one of the most gorgeous crystal-blue beaches in the world. I had a pocket full of money, a booming cocaine business, and a beautiful girlfriend, different than the one in Amsterdam. Materially, at this point in my life, it felt like I had everything in the world. Yet despite having everything I thought I wanted, as I looked out from that balcony to the beach below, I thought to myself, "If I jumped off of this balcony right now, the world would be a better place." A lump formed in my throat. And I cried.

Something inside of me was telling me that I would never feel happy and fulfilled pursuing purely selfish goals. At some level, I knew that life was about more than drugs and women and money, that true happiness comes from contributing to humanity. It's an evolutionary drive that motivates us all, and it's what led us from being Neanderthals to becoming civilized humans. Deep down, we all know we are connected to each other. We all want to make the world a better place.

After I returned from Cancun, my cocaine business started to spiral—and rapidly. Some other dealers from Miami stole $22,000 in cash from me. That $22,000 was supposed to pay off my drug connection, who had fronted me a kilo of cocaine for $22,000. I was able to collect $16,000 from people who owed me money from the last kilo, but I was still short by $6,000, and I decided to make up for it by selling twenty pounds of marijuana on the side. When the guy I sold the marijuana to showed up at the Roadhouse Grill with the money to pay me, he was wearing a wire. I had no idea. We had a couple of Long Island iced teas together, then went out to my car to do a couple bumps of cocaine. As a key full of cocaine went up my nose, seven police officers with bullet proof vests swarmed around my car, guns pointed, yelling, "Put your hands on the steering wheel! Right now!"

That same day, the feds questioned my then-girlfriend, who told them about eight kilos she drove up for me from Miami. In return for her cooperation, she wasn't charged with a crime. I was charged with conspiracy to distribute eight kilos of cocaine and 20 pounds of marijuana. By some twist of fate, I was released without bail, pending trial.

Here's where the lesson comes: because my drug dealing career was over, I was forced to re-evaluate my life. That's the thing about failure, tragedy, injury, or the death of a loved one. These things always force you to re-evaluate your life. The best thing I had going for me was a college degree and two years of law school under my belt. It just so happened that the last opportunity I had to register for law school classes was about to end.

I talked to the law school dean, who told me I'd still have a chance to become a lawyer. She told me about another convicted felon who had completed law school and became a member of the Bar. So, I registered for my last year of classes. It still boggles my mind that if I hadn't been busted right before the registration period was over, I never would have signed up for that last year of classes, and my opportunity to become a lawyer would have vanished. Even more surprising, when I pled guilty in federal court, the judge had enough wisdom and foresight to delay my sentencing until I had completed my degree. One week after I graduated from law school, I was sentenced to five years in prison.

Obviously, my career as a drug dealer was a colossal failure. But that failure was exactly what I needed. I needed it to learn those lessons to become the man I was destined to be. This is how failure works. It shows us what not to do, thereby clarifying what we *ought* to do. It shows us what we don't want so that we're sure of what we really desire. In this case, I learned that chasing pleasure, women, and money for selfish gain was a dead end, and that life is about contributing to the betterment of humanity and making the world a better place. Some people know this intuitively, but this was something I had to learn the hard way. I thank God every time I think about my arrest, because I have no idea what future my choices would have manifested if those circumstances hadn't forced me to stop dealing.

And I can't help but think about the timing of my arrest, just before my final opportunity to register for classes. Given all of the other things that fell into place and ultimately allowed me to finish law school, can I really write it off as coincidence? Like the Mercedes "coincidence?" Looking back, it's pretty clear that something much bigger was happening.

 Activity:

What would you consider your biggest failure?

_____
_____
_____
_____
_____
_____

What did it teach you about what you don't want?

_____
_____
_____
_____
_____
_____

What did it teach you about what you do want?

_____
_____
_____

_____

_____

_____

What did it teach you about who you don't want to be?

_____

_____

_____

_____

_____

What did it teach you about who you do want to be?

_____

_____

_____

_____

_____

How did it show you the wrong way of getting what you want?

_____

_____

_____

_____

_____

What did it teach you about the right way to get what you want?

_____
_____
_____
_____
_____

CHAPTER 5

THE POWER OF BELIEFS

When the law school dean told me the story of the other convicted felon that became a lawyer, that was a critical moment for me. It established in me the core belief that becoming a lawyer was an attainable goal. Core beliefs are beliefs we hold about life itself. Some of the most important core beliefs are the ones we hold about what is possible for us. If I hadn't believed the goal of becoming an attorney was attainable, I never would have pursued it. Beliefs give rise to thoughts. Thoughts give rise to emotions. Emotions give rise to decisions. Decisions give rise to actions. And actions result in consequences. It all starts with core beliefs.

The individual who has achieved self-mastery regularly examines their own beliefs to determine which ones are empowering and which ones are disempowering. They discard the disempowering beliefs and enhance the empowering beliefs. This is a lifelong process, and it's not a one-size-fits-all proposition. The most important thing is to first ask yourself, and then examine the answer to this question: "Who am I in relation to the rest of the universe?"

This is not a book about religion. Obviously, there are successful people in every religion, and there are successful people who choose no religion whatsoever. My suggestion for people who are religious is to start where you are and examine your own beliefs within the framework of the religion that you follow. Every religion has aspects that support a belief in the power of the self. Almost every religion teaches methods of self-empowerment. Christianity, for instance, teaches that with faith one can move mountains. Toaism teaches that the entire universe supports our goals as long as we act in alignment with our true self. Focus on the empowering aspects of your religion, and constantly examine the results that follow.

As master of the self is a master of self-reflection. They pay attention to their own thought processes and listen to the voice inside their head. When they encounter a negative thought, they take a hard look at it and attempt to root out the cause. Negative thoughts are always the result of a disempowering core belief. When someone who has achieved self-mastery identifies a disempowering core belief, they go to work on discarding that belief by replacing it with an empowering one. They repeat the empowering belief over and over until it becomes a new thinking habit. It's easier said than done, but when it's done systematically, the master of the self will see massive changes in their life.

An example of a disempowering belief:

I barely graduated from high school. I suffered from the core belief that I was less intelligent than other people. I thought I was slow, and so did a lot of folks. I remember coming home from school as a child and crying to my parents, telling them, "I'm stupid. I'm just stupid." I hung on to the belief because it was comfortable. It was easy. I had no plans to go to college, because I didn't think I was smart enough. If I had admitted to myself that I was smart, I wouldn't have had any excuses for why I was such a slacker. Instead of going to college, I got a job making Egg McMuffins at McDonald's in the mornings, and a second job making Whoppers at Burger King at night for $3.65 an hour. I had zits all over my face from cooking with grease, and even though I was working almost eighty hours a week, I wasn't even making enough money to pay my car insurance and put gas in my station wagon, which was leaking oil and rusting so bad you could see the ground through the floorboard. Those kinds of difficulties are enough to make anybody re-examine their core beliefs.

My mom was worried about me, so she bought me a set of cassette tapes by Brian Tracy called *The Psychology of Achievement*. I started listening to those tapes every day as I commuted back and forth from work. Brian Tracy encouraged me to throw out any negative beliefs about myself and to replace them with goals instead. He said that, when you're trying to figure out what you want to do with your life, you have to ask yourself, "What would I do if I knew I could not fail? If I was guaranteed success in any endeavor, what would I choose?"

At first, being a lawyer was so far out of the realm of possibility that I didn't even consider it. But after listening to the tapes over and over, I started to daydream. The lawyers I saw on TV shows always looked so cool—they wore expensive suits, got all of the pretty girls, and made a bunch of money. "If I was guaranteed success in any endeavor," I thought, "I would be a lawyer."

And I made that my goal. I registered for community college, and breezed through a bunch of remedial classes, getting myself ready for college level courses. Because I knew that getting into law school required good grades, I started making straight A's in my college classes. I ended up graduating from the University of Central Florida with a 3.64 GPA and getting accepted into Florida State University Law School. After graduating from law school, I scored in the top 10% on all three sections of the bar exam, competing against people from Harvard, Yale, and other top-notch Ivy League schools. I completely obliterated my disempowering core belief that I was slow.

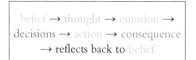

belief → thought → emotion → decisions → action → consequence → reflects back to belief

More importantly, if I had hung onto that core belief, as most people do, I would probably be working some menial job with little pay and less fulfillment.

 Activity:

Questionnaire, identifying beliefs: Rate the following beliefs 1-5, 5 most identifies with the statement.

1. I am not great or able to make good decisions. _____
2. I am not able to deal with most situations. _____
3. I am not smart enough. _____
4. I need others more than they need me. _____
5. I have failed more than I have succeeded. _____
6. I am not safe and could easily be taken advantage of. _____
7. I am less worthy than most others. _____

8. I am trapped in my current situation. _____

9. There is something wrong with me. _____

10. I love others more than they love me. _____

11. I find it difficult to make new friends. _____

12. I don't like how i look. _____

13. I am the last person friends/family call if they need help. _____

14. I am different than everyone else. _____

15. I am not worthy of success. _____

15-30 (I can work on a few things, but otherwise I'm happy with who I am)

30-45 (I have some work to do because there are some areas that are certainly holding me back)

45-75 (I really need to address my beliefs about myself because they are not leading me to success)

CHAPTER 6

CLAIM YOUR POWER

As a personal injury lawyer, my job is to help people who have been seriously hurt, many of whom are suffering the most difficult period of their lives. Over the years, I have represented thousands of people who are facing overwhelming challenges. I've witnessed firsthand the way some people rise to their challenges and the way others fall deeper into misery and defeat. My experience as a personal injury lawyer has given me important insights into my fellow humans. I've noticed that, with the right guidance, many people who appear destined to fail end up wildly successful. It's shocking to see how many people out there have never had ANY guidance when it comes to triumphing challenges. They allow themselves to be defeated, completely blind to the fact that in their greatest challenge lies their greatest opportunity.

Most of my clients have been seriously injured due to no fault of their own—typically something like a rear-end collision, where my client could do nothing to prevent the crash. When this happens, the client often feels like the victim of circumstance, powerless in a world that is mostly beyond their control. In extreme cases, they might suffer from post-traumatic stress disorder, which is a mental illness that can cause people to relive a traumatic event in a way that's beyond their control. Post-traumatic stress is very real. It results in anxiety, depression, and a feeling of "why bother?" Some of my clients who are suffering the most end up missing medical appointments and losing their jobs. Their lives spiral even further out of control, and they look to their personal injury case as a lifeline. "When my case settles," they think, "I will gain back control of my life."

Ironically, the clients who are waiting for a settlement to save them have the least chance of a successful outcome—it's ironic because they are often the clients who are suffering the most. From a practical standpoint, this problem arises because these clients miss the medical appointments that could potentially improve their physical condition. They sometimes refuse medical treatment, they refuse to see a counselor for PTSD, they refuse pain management injections that could help get them back to work sooner, and they refuse to get back to work when they can and should. The net result is that my client ends up worse off than they could have had if they had committed themselves to bettering their situation.

The clients who end up with the best results are the ones who are determined to be the heroes of their own stories. Despite all evidence that some things in life are out of our control, the client decides he or she is going to take control of his or her life. This concept doesn't just apply to personal injury victims. The number-one most important factor in predicting somebody's future success or failure is this: is this person taking full responsibility for their own life? On one side of the success spectrum are people who feel like victims of circumstance. On the other side are people who feel like the masters of their own destinies. The people who believe themselves to be masters of their own destinies are the ones who will inevitably succeed.

However, even those people only reach their greatest potential by actually becoming the masters of themselves. It sounds as easy as saying, "I am the master of my own destiny," but it's not. There is a huge difference between believing you are the master of your own destiny and actually becoming it. In the following pages, I'll share with you the keys to self-mastery that, if used consistently, will allow you to live your greatest life.

I realize we touched on this in the last chapter, but it's worth repeating. The first key to becoming your greatest self and living your greatest life is this: committing yourself to a lifelong practice of self-empowerment, developing and nourishing empowering core beliefs. The degree to which you feel in control of your life is directly related to the amount of control you experience, and the more powerful you feel, the more powerful you are. This is a very interesting concept because it isn't uncommon for human beings to experience circumstances that, by all counts, appear to be out of our control. Take, for example, my client who gets crashed into by a drunk semi-truck driver, causing catastrophic injuries. How can I, a personal injury lawyer who has seen countless of these accidents, argue that our lives are completely within our control?

Because I have seen it with my own eyes. Life sometimes throws us curveballs we never expect. That's reality. I'm not pretending that we can consciously control every single aspect of our lives, but we can ALWAYS control where we're headed. We can always control how we respond to our circumstances, and we can ALWAYS find ways to turn our greatest challenges into our greatest opportunities. I have a client who was paralyzed from the neck down in a motorcycle accident who is now walking around with full use of his arms and legs. He has an entirely new perspective on life and wakes up every day grateful for his ability to use his arms and legs. I have another client who, despite being paralyzed from the chest down, has become a better husband, a better father, and a better member of his community who actively tries to make this world a better place.

Developing a core belief that we have 100% control over the most important aspects of our lives is critical to success. Stephen Hawking might still be the greatest scientific mind of all time, even though he was trapped in a wheelchair with zero ability to use his arms and legs. Some people might argue that his inability to use his body compelled him to use his mind, and that if he hadn't suffered from severe multiple sclerosis, he might have never contributed so much to the scientific community and the world itself. Despite a life of physical limitation and constant pain, Hawking is famous for saying how lucky he was to live the life he lived! He couldn't control the disease he suffered from, but he controlled how he reacted to it. He controlled his attitude toward it, and he controlled his destiny by turning his diseased and trapped body into an opportunity to develop his mind and become a legend in his own time. Even after his death, he continues to serve as an amazing example of what's possible for anyone who chooses to take control of his or her own destiny.

 Activity:

Whether or not you are currently, or recently going through a traumatic event, which statement most identifies with you?

Are you the a) sit back and wait, or b) a self-motivated, take every opportunity to improve, kind of person?

_____

Considering your answer to the above, do you believe you are, and act, like the master of your own destiny? Explain.

_____
_____
_____
_____
_____

CHAPTER 7

THE POWER OF WHY

One of the most important core beliefs you can address is the answer to the question, "Why am I on this earth?" Most people never dare to answer this question because it's scary to even think about. Just saying, "What is the purpose of life?" can bring up so many conflicting ideas and thoughts. Many people are afraid to even speculate because they are afraid of getting it wrong or being criticized by other people who think they know better. However, having the courage to answer this question makes the difference between high achievers and average performers. High performers ask themselves the question, "Why am I here?" over and over. They are constantly thinking about and tweaking their own answer to the question, and they live a life of purpose.

Again, the answers may vary: there isn't a one-size-fits-all approach. My beliefs about why we are here are not necessarily the same as yours, nor should they be. Every person's "why" is unique to them. Whatever you choose as your "why," my suggestion is to make it something that pumps you up, that makes your heart race, that inspires you to be your greatest self. We are not put on this earth to be the victims of circumstance, blown this way and that way by winds too powerful for us to resist. Every single human being is an intricate part of the whole and has ultimate power over their own reality. By answering the question, "Why?" you will reveal to yourself your true purpose and give yourself the power to act in alignment with it and achieve whatever it is you think you are here to achieve. That's where your real power arises.

Most people have heard of "The Butterfly Effect," the notion that the flap of a butterfly wing on one side of the planet can affect the weather on the other. The idea is that tiny changes in conditions can create huge changes in the mathematical equation we call reality. It was first popularized in the 1800s in Johann Gottlieb Fichte's book, *The Vocation of Man*, which theorized that, "You could not remove a single grain of sand from its place without thereby changing something throughout all parts of the immeasurable whole." At the time of the writing of *The Vocation of Man*, physicists had not yet proven that everything is connected. And it took them over one hundred years to do it. In 2012, Peter Higgs and Francois Englert proved the existence of the Higgs field, which is a field of energy that connects everything in the universe. The discovery of the Higgs field won them the Nobel Prize, and it not only corroborated the Butterfly

Effect theory—it explained it. Everything that happens in the universe, no matter how small, affects everything else, because it is all connected.

How does this apply to our lives? Every single thing we do affects all of existence! I'm going to come back to this subject and explore it more in depth in a later chapter, but here's the gist: Every thought we have, every emotion we feel, every breath we take, every step we make changes the entire equation of reality forever, not just in small ways, but in massive ways we can't even imagine. If the flap of a butterfly wing in the United States can change the weather in Australia, imagine how powerful a human being can be with focused intent. This is precisely why our core beliefs are so important: because our core beliefs give rise to thoughts, which give rise to emotions, which give rise to actions, which result in real consequences.

Most people never understand their true power. They believe that if they lie, cheat, or steal—or if they cut someone off in traffic—the results are minimal. It's no big deal. They think that if they are kind to someone who needs their help, the benefits of their kindness are limited solely to the person they are helping. The reality, however, is that everything we do has ripple effects that reverberate throughout time and space. Everything we do affects everybody else. The answer to the question, "Why?" allows us to direct this amazing power toward something that is personally meaningful. When we start to live in alignment with our "why," we experience the fulfillment of living a life of purpose. So far in my life, I have experienced no greater joy than feeling that I'm doing exactly what I'm supposed to be doing for all the right reasons.

 Activity:

7 layered WHY development exercise:

What do you want to do?

_____

_____

Why is that important to you?

_____

_____

Why is that important to you?

_____

_____

Why is that important to you?

_____

_____

Why is that important to you?

_____

_____

Why is that important to you?

_____

_____

Why is that important to you?

_____

_____

CHAPTER 8

How Do You Discover Your Mission in Life?

Your life's mission should be something that fires you up. It should be so exciting that you don't need to muster the motivation to pursue it. You are driven by it. You can't help but to pursue it. You are so completely obsessed with accomplishing your mission that almost nothing else matters. The thought of your mission keeps you up at night and wakes you up early each morning. It makes you happy. You have never been happier than when you have made progress toward accomplishing your mission.

There are four elements that will guide your mission in life: fire, air, water, and earth. The first element is fire. You need a fire in your belly that drives you forward without you even having to step on the gas. The key to discovering your fire element is to look at the most painful experiences of your life, the biggest challenges you have overcome. We have all faced adversity. We have all lost. We have all failed. The pain from those losses, that adversity, that failure becomes fire energy we can use to propel us on our journey toward accomplishing an amazing mission.

John Walsh is a perfect example of somebody who used the most painful experience of his life as the fire he needed to pursue an important mission. His son, Adam, was murdered by a serial killer when Adam was only six years old. After two weeks of searching, Adam's severed head was found in a drainage canal in Indian River, Florida. Serial killer, Ottis Toole, confessed to the crime, but was never convicted of it due to loss of evidence and a recanted confession, despite being convicted of other murders. Adam's murder created a fire in John Walsh's belly that drove him to start the television program "America's Most Wanted," dedicated to helping law enforcement officers track down bad guys and put them behind bars. "America's Most Wanted" became wildly successful and ultimately led to the arrest of hundreds of dangerous criminals. There is no way to tell how many lives John Walsh saved by getting murderers and criminals off the streets.

The second element to discovering your mission in life is air. The key to your air element is examining your talents. What do you love to do? What kind of activities are you drawn to without having to put in an effort? We all have at least one talent that seems to come extremely easily to us. There is a reason why we have that talent. We are supposed to use it.

That brings us to the third element—water. We attain our water element when we use both our air and fire elements to create an energy that flows toward the benefitting the greater good. The idea is to take the knowledge, wisdom, and energy we've gained from our most painful experiences, combine them with our natural talents, and use them to improve the lives of other people. John Walsh was building luxury hotels when his son was murdered, but he had a particular talent for organizing and motivating people. He combined that talent with the fire in his belly fueled by the murder of his son, and he changed the world.

The final key to pursuing your mission is your earth element. The idea is to take the fire, air, and water elements and bring them down to earth by centering your mission around a master goal. John Walsh's mission, for example, was to get bad guys off the street and make the world a safer place. He brought that mission down to earth with the goal of creating a highly successful television show dedicated to helping the police catch criminals.

How do you bring your fire, air, water, and earth elements together? There are a million different ways, but the best way I have found is to spend time sitting in silence. Some people read a religious text. Some people jog. Other people walk. Others yet beat a drum. I've heard of others who like to spend time alone listening to classical music or techno music.

While I was in prison, I decided my mission in life was to become a lawyer and partner in a law firm. However, at that time, I didn't have a clear understanding of why I wanted those things on a deeper level. I thought my goals were about being successful, making money, and getting pretty girls. Only later, after I had been a lawyer for three years, did I discover what I really wanted. I want to share an experience I had that allowed me to really clarify my mission in life.

In 2008, when I had my first daughter, Sophia, I had a deep desire to become a better man. I was obsessed with discovering the purpose of life and finding out why we are here. Around the time of Sophia's first birthday, I started reading a book by Deepak Chopra entitled, *The Book of Secrets*. I listened to the audio version several times. What I loved about *The Book of Secrets* is that it doesn't try to tell you the keys to the universe, but rather it encourages you to unlock them by figuring things out for yourself.

Deepak is a big proponent of meditation, so I decided to meditate in my car while waiting in a church parking lot for a meeting. I had meditated before, but I never really thought it was helping me in any way. I had never tried the OM meditation, which involves chanting the sound "OM." Before meditating, I decided to get in the right frame of mind by saying a prayer. "I don't know what to call you," I said. "I don't know what to believe. But whatever power there is that controls this universe, show me what I am supposed to do."

I stayed there meditating for what seemed like about twenty minutes. During that twenty minutes, I felt the most amazing sensation I had ever experienced in my entire life. The feeling was not of this world—the best way I can describe it is full-body ecstasy. My whole body started tingling and it felt like my mind had opened. As I sat there, breathless, a rush of ideas poured into my mind. I was in a heightened stated of awareness, where I was able to piece together a lot of what I had learned about life and humanity up until that moment. I could see the meaning and purpose behind life itself. I understood clearly that humanity had evolved from single-celled organisms into amazingly complex, self-aware human beings. I could see that there was a clear pattern of evolution, whereby outdated organisms had given way to more adaptable and more intelligent species. And I realized that human consciousness has continued to evolve, to the extent that we are becoming more self-aware, more knowledgeable, and more powerful every moment of every day. In my mind's eye, I could see how we as a species could either use our amazing knowledge and power to destroy ourselves, or to transform this world into an absolute paradise. I felt a deep desire to contribute to the positive evolution of humanity: I wanted to do my part to make the world a better place.

Then I began to understand how my own life had evolved. By that time, I was already a partner in a well-established law firm. I could see how my time in prison had given me the tools to overcome major challenges, and how it had taught me the value of overcoming challenges. I understood how the helplessness and fear I suffered in prison had driven me to reclaim my power. I never wanted to feel powerless again. And I didn't want anybody else to feel powerless either. I realized how poetic it was that I had become a personal injury lawyer, whose profession is based upon helping people who are going through some of the most difficult challenges in their lives. When somebody crashes into a client's car and causes major injuries, they often feel powerless, just like I did in prison. I knew then that my mission in life was to make the world a better place by empowering people to overcome challenges and come back stronger.

All of this happened while I was sitting in my car, tingling all over, breathless. As I caught my breath, I knew in my heart that my life would never be the same.

Activity:

Fire: The most painful experiences in your life:

_____
_____
_____
_____
_____

Air: Your talents, what you love to do, what you're drawn to, that comes easy to you:

_____
_____
_____
_____
_____

Water: Take the knowledge, wisdom and energy from fire and air (painful experiences + natural talent) and use them to benefit others:

_____
_____
_____
_____
_____

Earth: Take your painful experiences + talent + for the benefit of others and ground them with a master goal:

_____
_____
_____
_____
_____

CHAPTER 9

CREATE A MISSION STATEMENT

Super successful people are always on a mission. The most successful people in the world not only know why they are here, but they have written it down and made it into a mission statement. Oprah Winfrey, Bill Gates, Sheryl Sandberg, Michael Jordan, Elon Musk, Jack Welch, Steve Jobs, Warren Buffet—all of them have distilled life's mission down to a single sentence. That mission statement becomes the cornerstone of their business empires, and is disseminated and used by every employee who works for their business. The mission statement helps them focus and informs all of their decisions. One of the most powerful exercises a person can do for themselves is to create a very clear mission statement, write it down, repeat it often, and live by that mission statement every day.

Mission statements aren't just helpful for businesses. They can transform the life of every person on earth. A mission statement should be stated in one sentence, in plain language that's easy to remember and repeat. A personal mission statement, as opposed to a corporate mission statement, should start with the words, "My mission in life is to..." For instance, my mission statement is:

My mission in life is to empower people to overcome challenges and come back stronger.

If anyone ever asks me my purpose in life, I can tell them in an instant.

I encourage everyone reading this book to write down a mission statement right now. This will absolutely change your life. There is no right or wrong answer, and you are free to revise your mission statement a million times if you desire. The important point is to decide on a mission and start moving forward. Once you have a clearly defined mission, you can start setting goals that help you accomplish the mission you've set out for yourself. Goals are how you measure and monitor your success in pursuing your mission.

 Activity:

Use the previous Fire/Air/Water/Earth exercise to develop mission statement. It should begin......

My Mission in life is _____

_____
_____
_____
_____

How does your mission statement make you feel?

_____
_____
_____
_____
_____

CHAPTER 10

DECONSTRUCTING DREAMS AND VISIONS

Our subconscious mind is always guiding us by giving us ideas and directing our attention to the things in our environment that will help us achieve our greatest desires. One of the best ways to find your purpose in life and to pursue your goals is to be on the lookout for anything that continues to attract your attention. Pay attention to synchronicities, coincidences, and repetitive thoughts because they are often the result of your subconscious mind trying to lead you in a certain direction—I also recommend paying attention to dreams. As the following story illustrates, the subconscious mind is always working toward our benefit.

In 2008, my third year as a lawyer, I earned a bunch of money. I thought it was all the money in the world, so I started spending as if it would never run out. I only paid about half of what I should have paid in quarterly taxes. I figured I would make up for it in 2009, before the April 15 deadline. Well, 2009 turned out to be a bad year for the firm, and I only made about $60,000 total. $60,000 wasn't nearly enough to pay for the new house, my wife's new BMW, and our new Lexus SUV, let alone the $65,000 tax debt. 2010 was a decent year, but not nearly enough to get us out of the hole I had dug. In 2011, my wife's BMW got repossessed, my house was facing foreclosure, and the IRS froze my personal bank account. I had to borrow money from my sister-in-law to afford diapers for my infant twins. I borrowed money from my senior partner so I could purchase a cheap used car.

Fast forward to November of 2011. Our situation hadn't improved much. In fact, was grim. My fellow partners had asked to see my financials. I thought they might be ready to kick me out of the partnership. I decided I would wash cars, wait tables, do whatever I had to do to help us get through this. One night—it was November 11th—my wife and I had a long, heart-to-heart talk. We agreed that so long as we were together as a family, we would be happy, even if we had to live in a cardboard box. We hugged each other and cried together, and I felt the worry I had been carrying around release.

That very night, I had a dream that changed everything. Before I share this story, let me address the people who might write it off as "just a dream." This particular dream had real-life consequences, the kind of consequences most people only dream about, pardon the pun. But the dream itself is not the point. The point is how my subconscious mind led me to a resolution for my financial problem.

The dream seemed as real as any waking experience I've ever had. I was standing in the middle of a loud stadium full of cheering people, preparing to walk across a stage and accept a diploma. To my right were my mom and dad, and to my left was the most evil, selfish person I had ever known in my life. I'd grownup with this woman. She had been emotionally abusive to me as a child. I had been carrying around a deep hatred for her my entire life.

"What are you doing here?" I said.

She looked at me with the most loving, compassionate expression, and she said, "I love you so much. I'm part of your soul family, and I've always been with you. I came to earth to play the role of an evil person, so that you could learn the lessons you needed to learn to become the man you've become. I am so proud of you."

She hugged me, and I could feel the love emanating from her. I sunk into her arms and started sobbing.

When I woke from the dream, I was still sobbing like a child—real tears. It woke my wife, who sat up and held me in her arms for about an hour while I cried. As the tears flowed, I tried to process what the dream meant to me. I could feel something changing inside of me.

Fast forward to later the next evening, when I suddenly experienced the worst headache of my life. It felt like laser beams were cutting grooves into my brain. I went to the emergency room and got a Toradol injection, which did nothing for the headache. The pain lasted all night long and into the next morning. I got zero sleep. The next day I went back to the emergency room. They couldn't help me. I was beyond miserable. I went back home to suffer through the pain. Finally, I decided to meditate in my bedroom. I told my wife, "I'm locking this door. Please do not let anybody touch it."

I laid myself down to meditate and, very quickly, I felt an energy field surround my body like a cocoon. I heard a voice in my head. It wasn't audible, but more like a very powerful thought. "This is your cocoon," it said. "When you come out of it, your consciousness will have ascended." I don't usually hear voices. This was not something that had ever happened to me before.

I decided I wasn't going to move. The next thing you know, I found myself in another realm, like a dream realm, but it was more like I was having a vision. This was a very interesting experience, because I was conscious of being in the other realm while at the same time meditating in my bed. The other realm seemed to be set during the medieval times. I was standing on a bridge by a castle, watching two soldiers as they stood guard over a building on the other side. They opened the double doors to the building, and out of the building came a huge cloud of black smoke. The smoke filled the double doorway, and I could see the forms of human bodies floating within the smoke. It was coming toward me as I stood on the bridge. One of the medieval soldiers walked up to my face and said in a deep authoritative voice, "It's time to release this." The smoke began to funnel into my chest. I could feel this black energy going inside my heart and coming out of my head.

Meanwhile, I was still conscious of myself meditating in bed, my entire body trembling as this was happening. As the black cloud of energy escaped through the top of my head, I could feel myself releasing all of the anger, resentment, jealousy, regret, and psychological pain I had carried with me throughout my life. I was able to forgive not only the evil person who had been in my dream, but also anyone who had ever done me wrong, and anyone who had ever done anybody wrong. I completely accepted life exactly as it is, and I was able to let go of all of the judgment I had lived with. At the end of the vision, I heard the voice of one of the medieval soldiers saying, "Congratulations. You just released all of your self-defeating programs."

When I opened my eyes and came out of the meditation, my headaches were gone. Not only that, I felt ecstatic, and for the next twenty-four hours, it felt like I was walking on air. That very week, my partners settled some cases, and I made $600,000 in personal income. That money completely wiped out my IRS debt, paid off the debt on my house, and I have been beyond prosperous ever since.

Most people accept that dreams are the product of our subconscious mind. To me, dreams are the best evidence of the mind's ability to create new realities. I've had dreams, like the graduation dream, that seemed as real as any experience I've ever had while awake. Some of those dreams took me to places I had never consciously imagined—they teleported me to other planets, allowed me to fly over the most amazing landscapes, and introduced me to interesting people like Jesus and Angelina Jolie. Of course, I'm not alone in this. Almost everybody has varied and interesting dreams, and lots of people have had dreams with full sensory experiences. If our minds are powerful enough to create these realities in full color and with full sensory experience, what else are our minds able to do?

I believe, as do many psychologists, that when the subconscious mind communicates with the conscious mind, it tends to communicate with symbols and metaphors, so it can relay a lot of information in a short time period. Dreams typically last 5 to 20 minutes, but we can usually only remember them in tiny bits and pieces. The parts we remember hold the key to the message that our subconscious mind is trying to bring to the surface. For instance, when the evil person in my graduation dream said, "I came to earth to play the role of the evil person so that you could learn the lessons you needed to learn to become the man you've become," that was the message my subconscious mind wanted to relay. The evil person in the dream symbolized all the evil in the world. The dream wasn't about her at all. It was about understanding that the obstacles placed in our path—such as, in my case, this evil person—can serve to teach us the lessons we need to learn in order to become the people we desire to become.

The vision with the medieval soldiers and black smoke symbolized the release of dark energy from my consciousness. My entire life, I had held onto anger and resentment toward people I believed had done me wrong and all of the injustices I perceived in the world. Despite the fact that I had hurt a lot of people in my life, I was very quick to judge people for hurting others. I was angry about all the murderers, rapists, school shooters, robbers, and anyone in general who committed violent and selfish acts. Never the mind the fact that I was a convicted felon and former drug dealer. I was brutal in my hypocrisy. I even judged people for judging other people—and I judged myself for judging. It was a vicious cycle. The dream and vision symbolized the release of all of that baggage.

One fascinating part of the vision was the end, when I heard the soldier's voice saying, "Congratulations. You just released all your self-defeating programs." What an amazing revelation! Never in my life had I thought of anger, resentment, judgment, and self-judgment as "self-defeating programs." The term fascinated me. Our minds are very much like computers, and the reality we experience is determined by the programs we allow to operate in the background of our minds. My subconscious mind was telling me that anger, resentment, and judgment had been holding me back from achieving my goals of helping as many people as I could overcome injuries and come back stronger. I was angry at all of the evil-doers in the world, because I saw myself as separate from them. I thought I was better than them. I felt no connection to them. I was buying into the exact same energy that caused them to do evil acts. How fascinating is it that I was able to release these programs in one fell swoop, and immediately realized a huge financial windfall that changed my entire life!

Always remember that your subconscious mind is working for your benefit 100% of the time. In the next chapters, I'll discuss how our subconscious minds are connected to the consciousness of every other person on the planet, and therefore know the most efficient way for us to reach our goals. If you pay attention to repetitive thoughts, dreams, signs, and symbols you come across throughout the day, you can shorten the time frame by which you reach your goals and can achieve exponentially more with much less effort.

Activity:

For the Next 3 days track your dreams. You may not have any, but if you do, or think you do, write any thoughts here:

Day 1.) _____
_____
_____
_____
_____

Day 3.) _____
_____
_____
_____
_____

Day 2.) _____
_____
_____
_____
_____

CHAPTER 11

PUTTING THE PIECES TOGETHER

The experience I had while meditating in my car, winning the silver Mercedes convertible, and the vision of the black smoke led me to ask some serious questions. Was I crazy? Were these experiences just coincidences? What was really going on here?

The Mercedes experience was extremely puzzling, because there didn't appear to be a cause and effect relationship between me wanting the Mercedes and getting the Mercedes. I didn't plan to go to a Mercedes Club party, and I didn't expect a silver Mercedes SL500 to be there, but it happened. It seemed to be evidence that there was some power in the universe that was responding to my greatest desires. This was very personal. Somehow or another, and for whatever reason, the universe conspired to put me in the right place at the right time so that I would get that Mercedes. A lot of coordination and effort had to have gone on behind the scenes to make that happen. The Matchbox company had to make a Mercedes of the exact same make, model, color, and body as the one in my locker. My stepdad, who invited me to the party; the woman from the Mercedes club; and me—without knowing it, we were all somehow compelled, guided, or manipulated into doing what the universe wanted to get me that Mercedes.

Why me? Because we are all connected to one another in ways more intimate than most of us can imagine. Every person on this earth is part of a vast, interconnected network that makes up the collective consciousness of humanity. Every thought we have becomes part of the collective consciousness and influences everybody in the entire world. If a thought is repeated over and over with emotion, the rest of humanity is collectively influenced by it without even knowing it! This is the best explanation I can come up with for how that Mercedes manifested into my life the way it did.

The connection between minds is demonstrated beautifully in Ken Keyes's book *The Hundredth Monkey*. Here is an excerpt from the book:

The Japanese monkey, Macaca fuscata, had been observed in the wild for a period of over 30 years.

In 1952, on the island of Koshima, scientists were providing monkeys with sweet potatoes dropped in the sand. The monkeys liked the taste of the raw sweet potatoes, but they found the dirt unpleasant.

An 18-month-old female named Imo found she could solve the problem by washing the potatoes in a nearby stream. She taught this trick to her mother. Her playmates also learned this new way and they taught their mothers too.

This cultural innovation was gradually picked up by various monkeys before the eyes of the scientists.

Between 1952 and 1958 all the young monkeys learned to wash the sandy sweet potatoes to make them more palatable.

Only the adults who imitated their children learned this social improvement. Other adults kept eating the dirty sweet potatoes.

Then something startling took place. In the autumn of 1958, a certain number of Koshima monkeys were washing sweet potatoes -- the exact number is not known.

Let us suppose that when the sun rose one morning there were 99 monkeys on Koshima Island who had learned to wash their sweet potatoes.

Let's further suppose that later that morning, the hundredth monkey learned to wash potatoes.

THEN IT HAPPENED!

By that evening almost everyone in the tribe was washing sweet potatoes before eating them.

The added energy of this hundredth monkey somehow created an ideological breakthrough!

But notice.

A most surprising thing observed by these scientists was that the habit of washing sweet potatoes then jumped over the sea --

Colonies of monkeys on other islands and the mainland troop of monkeys at Takasakiyama began washing their sweet potatoes.

Thus, when a certain critical number achieves an awareness, this new awareness may be communicated from mind to mind.

Although the exact number may vary, this Hundredth Monkey Phenomenon means that when only a limited number of people know of a new way, it may remain the conscious property of these people.

But there is a point at which if only one more person tunes-in to a new awareness, a field is strengthened so that this awareness is picked up by almost everyone!

The story of the hundredth monkey effect has been criticized as being inaccurate and unscientific. Nevertheless, the critical components—that the isolated monkeys learned how to wash potatoes, and that monkeys on completely separate land masses were soon witnessed accessing the same skill—have been verified, and further scientific revelations such as the discovery of the Higgs Field and the Global Consciousness Project have confirmed that not only are monkey minds connected in a way we don't yet understand, but also that everything is connected.

When I had the vision of the black smoke in 2011, physicists were on the verge of proving that everything in the universe is connected by a unified field, a pervasive energy filling everything that exists. Physicists had long suspected that everything was connected, but until 2012, they didn't have conclusive proof. The idea had become a fundamental assumption to the theory of particle physics. The term Higgs Boson became the name for the theoretical elementary particle that pervades all that exists. Other physicists coined the term "God Particle," because of its omnipresent quality. From 1960 to 2012, physicists had sought to prove the existence of the God Particle. Physicists theorized that if the God Particle actually exists, they should be able to detect it by causing particle collisions at speeds so high that they could measure even the tiniest bit of energy affecting the particles when the collision occurred. On July 4, 2012, utilizing CERN's Large Haldron Particle Collider, physicists were able to prove by experiment that the God Particle does exist. In 2013, physicists Peter Higgs and Francois Englert were awarded the Nobel prize for the discovery of the God Particle. Everything in the universe is connected by this tiny particle.

The ramifications of the discovery of the God particle are staggering. If everything in existence is connected by a unified field, then it follows that all humans are connected by and to the unified field. And because humans are conscious, it follows that consciousness exists within the unified field, and that all of human consciousness is connected.

What blows me away is how the idea of the Higgs field helps explain what spiritual leaders and motivational speakers have been touting for centuries- that we are all connected. Christians are taught that God is omnipresent, everywhere and in everything. Jesus' admonition to, "Love thy neighbor as thyself," was more than just a platitude. It was acknowledgment that we are one with our neighbors. Taoists believe "we are all one with the Tao." The Tao is the energy that pervades everything. Hindus believe we are all part of the supreme creator, Brahma, and that Brahma exists in everyone and everything. Physicists have confirmed that, whatever name we choose to call it, there is an energy that lives within everyone and everything in this universe.

But there's more to the story here. In the pages that follow, I'm going to share with you how our connection to the universe works so you can harness the power of it to create the reality you most desire.

 Activity:

Let's retrace the last 4 steps that had to happen to bring you to this book to recognize the universe at work:

How did you physically get the book?

_____

_____

What circumstance led to meeting the person you got the book from or who recommended it?

_____

_____

What lead to meeting the person in #2?

_____

_____

What lead to meeting the person in #3?

_____
_____

CHAPTER 12

THE GLOBAL CONSCIOUSNESS PROJECT

If all of human consciousness is connected, it follows that the thoughts and emotions of every individual has an impact on the collective consciousness. Reality is a subjective experience of us interpreting data and information through our five senses. We interpret data through a lens of perception. That perception is formed by the collective consciousness of humanity. We tend to think of ourselves as individuals, but in reality, our thoughts, feelings, and perceptions are connected to the greater consciousness that makes up humanity. Everything we experience arises from the evolving collective. Our thought processes, our languages, our style, our likes and dislikes- everything that makes up the identity of each one of us is the product of the evolving consciousness of people who came before us and people who have influenced us in our lifetimes. Most of us have been molded mostly by our parents and teachers, who were molded and influenced by people before them, but in reality everyone that ever lived and is currently living has an impact on us in ways we can't even comprehend. If somebody in the past hadn't made up language, I couldn't write this book. The development of a language is a group effort, so therefore the collective who created the English language is part of who I am. If somebody else hadn't invented this computer I'm typing on, or the chair I'm sitting in, or the house I'm living in, I would not have been able to experience the reality I am currently experiencing. None of these things were created by an isolated individual. All of these things evolved over time as a result of a combination of thoughts of the human collective. Whether we know it or not, life is a group effort, and we are part of an evolving collective.

If a single person's thoughts have an impact on the collective consciousness, then a group of people who share the same thoughts can have an exponentially greater impact. I am a huge proponent of forming a mastermind group to amplify the power of our goalsetting process. A mastermind group is a group of people who meet regularly to discuss their goals and help each other formulate plans for accomplishing them. Only recently did I initiate a mastermind group, and I would say it is one of the most rewarding experiences of my life. Four or five of us meet every morning on a virtual Zoom meeting at 5:00 A.M. to discuss our goals and what we plan to do that day to move forward in attaining our goals. The power of the group mind coming together is something you have to experience to understand completely. My amazing group has motivated me and given me ideas I would never have otherwise conceptualized.

Scientists from Princeton University uncovered compelling and surprising evidence about the connection between humans and the amazing power of a unified group mind. They discovered that when large groups of people are thinking about the same event with heightened emotions, the group mindset can create coherent patterns from what would otherwise be a random sequencing of events. The scientists set up random number generating computers in 60 locations throughout the world, and they monitored the number patterns for more than twenty years. Basically, the machines generated ones and zeros randomly. Under normal circumstances, when measured over time, the ratio of ones to zeros would equal about 50/50, which is what one would expect from random number generators. However, the scientists found that when emotionally charged global events captivated a large portion of humanity, the random number sequences would suddenly become more coherent. They would produce a lot more ones than zeros, or a lot more zeros than ones.

For instance, when the terrorist attacks for September 11, 2001, happened, the entire world was focused on the horrific event. The random number generators suddenly began spitting out a lot more ones than zeros, so much so that the chances of the anomaly being the product random chance was only one in two thousand. Similar studies produced similar results with other events that captivated the attention of large portions of humanity at one time. For example, New Years Eve events consistently show an increase in coherence in the random number generators. Global meditation events also create coherence. At first, the scientists suspected these results were the product of random chance. But after studying the phenomenon and analyzing the data for more than twenty years, they've calculated that the possibility that the results are random is a trillion to one.

Some of the most fascinating results arise when analyzing data related to large group meditations. Although randomly occurring world events certainly create coherence in the field of potential, group meditations are even more likely to create such coherence. This is evidence that a unified group mind with specific intentions can be extremely powerful. This offers a possible explanation for the power of group prayer.

Humanity is afflicted with a false sense of disempowerment. None of us fully realize the full impact we have on the collective of humanity. Every thought we have influences the collective. Every action we take influences it even more. And the groups we create and the associations we form influence it even more. My hope is that the concepts that follow will enlighten the reader about the full extent of his or her amazing power.

 **Activity:**

What goes through your mind knowing you are connected to all other beings on the planet so closely? Do you feel more responsible for the choices you make?

_____
_____
_____
_____
_____

CHAPTER 13

Embrace the Reality of Infinite Possible Futures

We live in a world of infinite possible futures. Each one of us decides the future we will experience through the choices we make. I could choose right now to get up from my desk and get a glass of water. I could choose to walk out to my car, head to the airport, and fly to Hawaii. Or I could choose to stay here sitting at my desk, typing. And there are an infinite number of other choices I could make. Remember the Butterfly Effect. All of those choices have ripple effects that impact the entire universe. Each choice will lead me to an entirely different future.

Imagine an infinite number of doors surrounding you. Every door represents a possible choice you can make right now. You can only open one door at a time. With every door you open, with every choice you make, you step into an entirely different future. Every moment of every day we have an infinite number of possible choices, and therefore an infinite number of possible futures to choose from.

We experience our lives in a linear timeline, one moment after the other, and so on. The timeline we experience represents the story of our lives. Every moment represents a snapshot in time. A moment ago, the moment I am experiencing now existed only as a potential. One of a variety of possible futures becomes our present reality as each moment passes. The choices we make determine which future we experience as our present reality.

The idea of infinite possible futures becomes clear when thinking about pivotal moments in our lives. Sometimes I think about how my life would have been different if I had never taken the first ecstasy pill that inspired me to transform from law student to drug dealer. Before I was humbled by my prison experience, I never wanted to get married or have kids. If I hadn't gone to prison, I probably never would have met my wife, never would have married her, and I wouldn't have my three beautiful and amazing daughters. But where would I be now? There are an infinite number of possibilities, all of which existed as potentials before the fated moment when I took that first ecstasy pill.

Every moment of every day, we are composing the stories of our lives. Any future you can conceive in your mind and believe already exists as a possibility. The key to manifesting it as a reality is to stay focused on what you want and move forward as if the outcome has already been achieved. Remain open to your own inner guidance, and your subconscious mind can lead you to a future even better than you ever imagined.

As human beings, it's important to become aware of the infinite possibilities available to us, because we have the power to direct the flow of our conscious awareness. Every snapshot in time has an infinite number of possible focal points. We choose where to focus our attention. By directing our awareness with purpose and intention, we can choose a timeline where we experience excitement and joy or endless suffering—or anything in between.

Because there are an infinite number of timelines to choose from, every moment is a choice of monumental significance. And every thought we allow to surface in our minds represents a choice. Thoughts act like a steering wheel, shifting our trajectory every moment of every day. With a single thought, a person can shift timelines in an instant. The joyful person can become the sufferer, and the sufferer can choose a life of joy.

The future is a moving target. You might be headed toward one future, then, in a split-second, change directions and end up in another. Motivational speakers often discuss the importance of creating the reality you desire. In my experience, we don't actually create our reality: it's more accurate to say that we choose one over an infinite number of potential realities with the choices we make. Choosing a reality is like tuning into a radio station. There are countless programs already in existence, but you have to try a few signals that don't work to get to the station you want. You don't create the radio station, but by learning what you want and what you don't want, you tune into a station that is already available for your enjoyment. The same is true of potential futures. An infinite number of possible futures already exist. Our job is to choose which one we want—fully embracing the power of the infinite now is one of the most powerful ways of choosing it.

Every snapshot in time we experience is the now moment. Now is the moment of reckoning; now is the fulcrum of power. We all choose which future we experience by directing the flow of our conscious awareness in the now moment. As you read this book, you are choosing to focus your attention on improving your life instead of choosing to focus on something else. Every moment you choose to read this book, or any other book dedicated to improving yourself and your life, you are moving in the direction of a better future. You could be going in the opposite direction, thinking about your past and beating yourself up over bad choices you've made. You could be focusing on aches and pains in your body. You could be thinking about your fears, the economy, politics, whatever. There are an infinite number of things that could be commanding your attention. Yet the best way to choose the future reality you most desire is to embrace the power you have right now to choose the direction you want to move in, use your imagination to dream about what you really want out of life, and pursue your greatest desires.

Most people never do this. They operate on auto-pilot, going through the motions of life, but never stop to ask themselves the question, "What do I really want?" They never take the time to reflect on whether all of their activities are the best activities they could be choosing for themselves. And they never recognize their true power to choose their future. Instead, they spend a lot of time thinking about the things in life they can't control—whether it's the economy or the problems of their friends. Every moment they spend thinking about these things is a moment wasted, a moment where, instead, they could have seized the golden opportunity to focus on what they can control.

The truth is that every single person in the world can change their life instantly by making a decision right now about what they want and committing themselves to actualizing this new reality. A monumental moment in my life occurred when I decided to become a lawyer instead of working at a fast-food restaurant. Every successful person can trace their success back to a single moment that defined their lives or their careers. That moment always involves a decision they made with a firm sense of commitment. If you are not happy where you are, you can decide right now to go in a different direction.

In this way, every human being has unlimited power. Because we have the power to think and to focus our attention, we have the power to move in any direction we choose. We have the power to create thoughts with our imaginations that can expand both the quantity and quality of our possible futures. If Simone Biles never imagined herself being the greatest gymnast of all time, that future would not have become available to her. If Thomas Edison never thought that he could invent the first incandescent light bulb, we might still be reading by candlelight.

This book is about more than just overcoming obstacles. It's about navigating the sea of infinite possibilities. It's about choosing big, bold, awesome, and exciting timelines. It's about recognizing where we have been playing small and switching to a timeline that's worthy of the awesomeness that each and every one of us deserves to experience.

 Activity:

What is your current trajectory? - How does it play out?

_____
_____
_____

List 5 major decisions you have made in the last 10 years that could be considered "jumping timelines"

Jump 1: _____

Jump 1: _____

Jump 1: _____

Jump 1: _____

Jump 1: _____

CHAPTER 14

CREATE BIG, BOLD, AMAZING GOALS

When deciding your goals, be bold. Be brave. Think about what you would do if you had the entire universe supporting you, because it is. Remember that you are connected to everything, everywhere and at all times. The entire universe not only supports you, but it is also fully invested in you. The same energy that pervades every molecule in the universe also lives inside of you. You are a masterpiece of creation, the result of trillions of years of evolution. You are cutting edge technology, and you are still evolving. The evolution of your consciousness continues, and it continues to affect how the rest of the universe evolves. The universe is fully invested in your desire to reach your highest potential.

One of the keys to successful goal-setting is choosing a goal that, once achieved, will make the world a better place. Ask yourself, "What can I do that will have the greatest positive impact on the rest of the world?" This type of focus will ensure you have the wind at your back—there are evolutionary forces at work here. The world is trying to evolve in a positive way, and the best way to ride a horse is to travel in the direction it's headed. I realize that there are other negative forces at work in the world, but overall, the overall of our planet is trending toward a future of expanded awareness and a healthier, happier, and more technologically advanced global community. We've made it this far, and we have a long way to go. We can either move forward toward a better tomorrow, or we can choose to destroy ourselves. I'm on Team Better Tomorrow. I hope you are too.

The problem for many people is that their goals are too small. Little goals have little power. And they don't motivate people to act. Choose a goal that inspires you, that makes you excited—choose a goal that is so exciting it keeps you up at night just thinking about it.

Write Down Your Goals

One of the most powerful ways of moving toward your goals is to write down exactly what you want, in detail. The act of writing a goal programs the goal into your subconscious mind. The more often you write it, the stronger the programming, and the harder your subconscious mind goes to work on directing you toward a future where your goal is accomplished. When I created my goal of having the silver Mercedes SL 500 convertible, I wrote the goal down, and I got what I wanted. The fact that it came to me in a Matchbox size says something very important about how to write down your goals. Here's how I wrote it:

"I will own a silver Mercedes SL 500 convertible by December 31, 2005."

As written, my goal was absolutely realized. I wrote it down over and over, deepening the programming so that my subconscious mind could direct me to the future where my goal was actualized. I stated the goal in first person, as if it had already been accomplished. I gave the goal a deadline. These are all classic methods for effective goal setting.

But here's where I went wrong. I did not write the goal down in detail, as an experience. For instance, I could have written:

"It's December 31, 2005, and I am driving down 1-10 in a brand-new, silver Mercedes SL 500 convertible. The title, which is in my name, is in the glove compartment. The top is down. It's a beautiful, sunny day in Florida. The wind is blowing on my face. 'I Feel Good' is playing on the sound system. I am on top of the world!"

If I had written my goal down as a detailed experience, my subconscious mind would have had no choice but to direct me to a future where my goal was a reality. The more often I thought about it in detail, the more likely I'd be to actualize it exactly as I had imagined.

The second mistake I made was that I gave up. I put the Mercedes goal out of my mind because I became interested in something else, investing in real estate. It's curious to me that the real estate market collapsed shortly thereafter. If I had stayed focused on what I truly wanted and bought the Mercedes, I would have had the car of my dreams and avoided losing tens of thousands of dollars when the bottom fell out of the real estate market—not to mention the time and energy I'd lost investing in the real estate projects. I should have stayed focused on my goal. Lesson learned.

Begin Your Goal with the Words, "I Am."

The most powerful way to begin a goal is with the words, "I am." The words "I am," followed by a future scenario, cause your imagination to put yourself in the future you desire. The human brain cannot distinguish between an imagined scenario and a real one. To the human brain, imagination and reality are exactly the same. The brain also cannot distinguish between an imagined future reality and the present moment. Writing down the words "I am," followed by a future scenario, has the effect of tuning your subconscious mind into the reality you are imagining. The future reality you desire already exists as a potential. Your subconscious mind can direct you to it. The more often you tune into that future scenario by imagining yourself there, the more likely it is that it will manifest as a reality in your life.

One of my current goals is to build my law practice into a billion-dollar business. I'm determined to bring it to fruition, so as soon as this potential reality came to me, the first thing I did was write down a detailed scenario, in which the goal has already come to fruition:

It's December 31, 2029. I am sitting at my desk at the corporate headquarters of Fasig Brooks Law Offices, looking at the profit and loss statement for 2029. The statement shows more than a billion dollars in revenue and more than a thirty percent profit. I reflect on all of the lives we have changed over the years, all of the people we've helped overcome challenges and come back stronger over the years. My heart feels full and happy. Tears well up in my eyes. I am the largest shareholder of a billion-dollar law practice with offices throughout the United States, and I've done everything in my power to serve my clients and make this world a better place. I step out of my office into the sea of people I know and love, my law partners and all of the staff who have helped build this amazing business. Hundreds of us are bringing in the new year together. A waiter walks by, and I grab a champagne glass from his tray, move to the center of the room, and raise my glass for a toast. "Can I please have everyone's attention? Your attention, please. I want everyone here to know how much I love and appreciate you all, the people who have helped build this business, and the people who have stood by and supported us as we work so hard to serve our clients. Ten years ago, Dana and I set a goal of building this law firm into a billion-dollar business. At the time, we knew it wouldn't be easy. We knew there would be major challenges along the way, but we moved forward with the vision of changing as many people's lives as possible. Well, I'm holding in my hand a copy of the profit and loss statement for 2029, and I have some amazing news. As we set out to do ten years ago, Fasig Brooks has earned more than one billion dollars in revenue in 2029, which means that we collected more than three billion dollars for our clients nationwide. Over the last ten years, we have touched the lives of hundreds of thousands of people, many of whom were going through some of the biggest challenges of their lives. And we have succeeded not only in helping them get back to where they would have been if their injuries had never happened, but we have shown them how to come back stronger than ever. Thank you to all of you who have contributed to making this happen. Tonight, let's celebrate what we've accomplished. I thank God for each and every one of you."

This is how to create a future scenario that will actually occur. The plan is to read this scene out loud as many times as possible, and to take actions to make it happen. If I stay focused and replay this scene in my head enough, and if I replay it with enough emotion, the thoughts and emotions will motivate me to take the necessary actions, and nothing will be able to stop this scene from becoming a reality. I encourage the reader to write a similar scene where they are the hero of their own story, and the story climaxes at the point where they reach a master goal.

The Magic of Setting Deadlines

My experience with the five-year goals I set while I was in prison taught me the power and importance of setting deadlines. Since then, I have continued to set goals with deadlines, and over and over, I've seen how my goals almost always tend to come to fruition right before the stated deadline. To this day, I'm still dumbfounded by the fact that the Mercedes manifested itself in my life just days before December 31, 2005. The subconscious mind needs to be hardwired with information about the future we want in order to get us there. It works best when given specific dates. As Brian Tracy says, "A goal without a deadline is just a wish." Put a deadline on your wish, and it becomes a goal.

As much as I like the idea of creating five-year goals, it's also important to break them down into yearly goals, weekly goals, and daily goals. The most productive time of my life was a period when I wrote daily goals down every day on a three-by-five index card and carried it with me, crossing the goals off my list throughout the day as I accomplished them. Every Sunday, I'd re-read my five-year and yearly goals, and then I'd create weekly goals to push myself toward them.

The weekly and daily goals don't have to be as detailed as your long-term goals. They are more like to-do lists.

 Activity:

Developing your Goals-

5 year _____
_____

1 year _____
_____

1 week _____
_____

Today _____
_____

Create your I AM vision - see it, smell it, who is there, what does it look like, where is it, when is it, how do you feel?

_____
_____
_____
_____

CHAPTER 15

CREATE A MASTER GOAL

One difference between high achievers and people who accomplish very little is how far ahead they are able to visualize their futures. I'm encouraging the reader to set goals, but the reality is that all of us already are. Many people are worried about how they will get from one moment to the next and are wondering how they're going to get their next meal. I even have a close friend whose biggest goal is getting his next beer. Others still are striving to pay their rent every month and are focused on finding a place to live. They are all goal-driven people—but it's the high achievers who are looking further off into the future, beyond the confines and struggles of their daily lives.

I encourage everyone to create a ten-year goal, something that I call a master goal. This is a single goal that, if accomplished, will guarantee the accomplishment of your other, more short-term goals.

The master goal will become your way of quantifying and measuring the effectiveness with which you're pursuing your life's mission. What gets measured gets improved. A goal that cannot be quantified and measured is not a goal. Set the goal's deadline ten years into the future. Then, state the goal in a single, succinct sentence, using "I am" at the beginning and giving yourself a deadline at the end.

For instance, my master goal is, "I am the managing partner of a billion-dollar law firm by 1/1/2030." The moment I achieve that goal, all of my other goals will fall into place, and I will know beyond a doubt that I have succeeded in my life's mission, which is to help people overcome challenges and come back stronger. Since my law practice is focused on helping people do just that, if I succeed in building it into a billion-dollar business, I'll know that I have succeeded in a big way: I will have helped hundreds of thousands of clients. This book is part of my mission. I plan on giving it to every single client, past and present if I can find them.

One you've stated your master goal, write it down as many times a day as you can. Memorize it and repeat it to yourself every chance you get. Make it part of your identity, part of your inner dialogue. Whenever a challenge arises, as they do almost every single day, brush it off by repeating your master goal to yourself; similarly, whenever you find yourself thinking about petty things, redirect your focus and turn it toward your master goal.

If somebody cuts you off in traffic and you can't let it go, just pause for a moment, and say it out loud: "I don't have time to worry about that guy. I'm the managing partner of a billing dollar law firm by 1/1/2030."

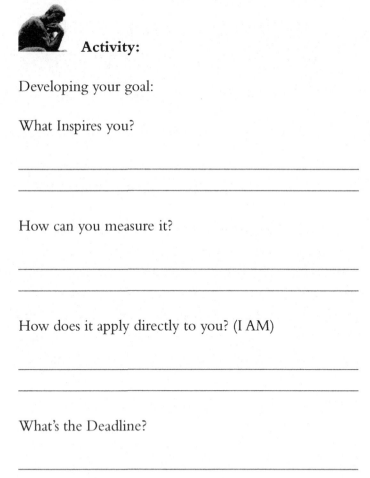 **Activity:**

Developing your goal:

What Inspires you?

_____

_____

How can you measure it?

_____

_____

How does it apply directly to you? (I AM)

_____

_____

What's the Deadline?

_____

_____

CHAPTER 16

BECOME THE PERSON YOU MUST TO ACHIEVE YOUR GOAL

If our lives are our stories, our character is everything. Have you ever noticed that there are certain types of people who seem destined to succeed at achieving their goals, whatever the goals may be, and others who seem destined to fail at whatever they do? Their success or failure depends not so much on what they do, but more on who they are. A lazy person, for example, is unlikely to build a successful business. Until that person changes who they are and becomes a highly energized, action oriented individual, they will struggle to achieve any degree of business success. Some people seem like naturally action-oriented, highly-energized people, while others don't. When setting goals, it's important to ask yourself the question, "What type of person do I have to be to achieve these goals?" Are you willing to become that person? If not, you might want to consider changing your goals.

If you are willing to put in the effort to become that person, you are destined to succeed. The first thing you need to do is write down the characteristics you need to develop in order to achieve the goals you have set for yourself. Write them down in first person as "I am" affirmations. For example, "I am focused. I am driven. I am a hard worker." You could attach your "I am" affirmation to an action such as, "I am a wake up at four in the morning and get to work guy." The important point is to create a list of characteristics that, if you possessed them, would guarantee your success. Constantly tell yourself you are that person, then act accordingly. Before you know it, you will become the person you described, and your success will follow naturally and easily.

Recognizing Your Highest and Best Self

We all have different aspects of ourselves that reveal themselves at different times in our lives. In moments of anger, we might show one side of ourselves; in moments of tenderness, we might reveal another. Each aspect of ourselves is whispering to us constantly, informing our thoughts and influencing our decisions.

Yet there is one part of ourselves that transcends all of them, and this represents our best and highest self. Your highest self has always been inside of you— you just might not have realized it.

Like the other aspects, it manifests itself as thoughts in your head. The most positive, loving, forgiving, and uplifting thoughts you think are coming from your highest self. Learning to recognize mine has been one of the most powerful endeavors I have ever pursued. Immediately afterward, I started noticing guidance from within that felt more loving, more empowering, and that was much more effective.

Your highest self loves you unconditionally, no matter what you say or do, and it keeps loving you even when other parts of you are filled with hate and regret. When you make a mistake, it is the voice inside of you that says, "I love you;" it is the voice inside that tells you, "Everything is going to be alright," and, "You'll do better next time." It doesn't encourage you to make the same mistakes, but gently guides you toward better decisions.

Now that I'm in tune with my highest self, every time I am visited by a memory or thought about something I regret, I can hear the words, "I love you," in my head. The thoughts are so powerful that sometimes I even say, "I love you," out loud without consciously choosing to say it. It just happens spontaneously sometimes, particularly when a challenging memory, a regret, or a resentment arises in my thoughts. Some people might think I'm crazy, and I probably am to some extent, but it feels good to know that there is a part of me that loves me unconditionally—and it feels good to recognize it.

Your Highest Self Forgives Everyone, Including You

It's tempting to think that if you love yourself unconditionally, you might continue to make the wrong decisions. However, the exact opposite is true. The more you love yourself, the better you are at making loving and thoughtful decisions. The mistakes we make in life are often born out of a lack of self-love, and your highest self loves you so much that your forgiveness is automatic. Learn to follow the guidance of your highest self, and you will make fewer mistakes and have much less to forgive yourself for. When I really dig down deep into the question of why I became a drug dealer during law school, the bottom line is I liked myself better when I was on ecstasy. I was more outgoing, funnier, wittier, and more confident when I was high. If I had loved myself unconditionally at that time in my life, I would never have felt the need to take a pill.

Your higher self also forgives anyone who makes a mistake, lies to you, cheats you, or betrays you. Your highest self wastes no energy on hate or revenge. Forgiving others is a challenge for many people. We all fear that if we are too quick to forgive, someone else will take advantage of us. However, forgiving somebody does not mean that you're giving them permission to treat you poorly. What I have found is that people will only treat you as poorly as you allow them. When you're following the guidance of your highest self, you love yourself too much to allow somebody to treat you in any way less than you deserve. Your highest self encourages you to set expectations. If somebody doesn't treat you well even after you've clearly specified your expectations, you'll still forgive them, but you'll no longer subject yourself to their abuse. Every relationship you form is a direct reflection of your relationship with yourself. If you love yourself enough, you will extricate yourself from abusive relationships, and your highest self will be the voice in your head encouraging you to do so.

Your Highest Self Knows You Can Achieve Anything

Have you ever wondered about that voice in your head that encourages you to think big and pursue your dreams? That's your highest self, too. Your highest self never doubts your ability to achieve your dreams. It knows you are worthy of everything good life has to offer and that you have something to offer that no one else in the entire world can do as well as you. And not only does it already know what that is; it's been trying to tell you your entire life.

If you're thinking, "I don't know what you want to do with my life," surrender it to your highest self, and pay attention to where your attention starts to lead you. You'll start noticing images, billboards, and TV commercials, or having thoughts or conversations that continue to lead you in that direction. This might sound like magic, but it's not. What's really happening is that you are opening your mind to your greatest possibilities—and in doing so, you're suddenly becoming aware of messages from your highest self that have always been there, but that you were missing because you weren't open to them.

Our highest selves are always trying to get our attention, but we often block the messages because we doubt ourselves or think they sound too good to be true. The fact is that we're limiting ourselves: we regularly sabotage our chances for success by not giving ourselves permission to pursue our highest goals. If we surrender to our highest selves, we allow those messages to rise into our consciousness and gain the courage to move forward toward our dreams without hesitation—but so long as we don't, we'll always continue to settle for less than what we deserve. When we allow our highest selves to take control, it tends to surprise us with circumstances that are far better than we had ever imagined.

An Epic Fail: How I Got onto America's Got Talent

The higher self makes no demands on you, but simply offers suggestions through loving thoughts. One thing I learned the hard way is that the voice of the higher self is a gentle whisper, but can be easily overpowered by the ego's desires. The higher self gently guides you to contribute to making this world a better place, but will allow you to fail if you go about it the wrong way, i.e. an egotistical way.

Remember the story about me meditating in my car, where I found out about my "why?" I was in a state of pure ecstasy, where I had a bunch of revelations about my purpose in life, and the purpose of life in general. I wanted to share what I felt with the world. I wanted other people to experience what I was feeling. I also wanted to share what I considered to be my newfound knowledge about how humanity has been evolving toward a higher state of consciousness. I had a deep desire to contribute to that continual evolution.

I came up with the idea of writing a rap song and trying out for America's Got Talent. I figured there was no faster and better way to reach the world with my message than by singing a rap song on national television. I thought that the best way to get onto the show would be to create a character, somebody fresh and new, somebody people would talk about. So I created the character Metatron, an angel of light sent to spread the message that humanity is evolving to a higher state of consciousness and to empower people to release the chains of limitation and create the lives of their dreams.

At the time, I didn't realize that my "why" was personal. I didn't have a monopoly on the one and only truth. There were other beliefs out there that were just as valid as my own, and I needed to learn to respect that before I could become as proficient as possible in my mission to help people overcome challenges and come back stronger.

So, I went to Atlanta and tried out for America's Got Talent. A huge group of talented and interesting people filled a huge auditorium. I met rappers, singers, dancers and contortionists, and I got to see several of them rehearsing their acts. As for me, I wore a white tuxedo with a white bow tie, and I was ready to introduce the world to Metatron, angel of light. I performed in front of three judges and was immediately granted a second audition. That evening, I did the second audition, and I was immediately informed that I had made it onto the show! I was pumped. I had no idea the entire experience would be a disaster.

In February of 2011, I went back to Atlanta. The producers asked me to give them a CD of the music I was going to use with my rap. Their protocol was to take the music and create something similar that they could register under their own copyright so as not to be sued for copyright infringement when they aired it on the show. I sent them my music, and they created a CD for me and set up an area where I could rehearse with the new music. I tried and tried, but I couldn't get the music to work with my rap. I would have had to write a completely new song, only there wasn't any time. By the time they called me out to the stage, I was panicking. I wanted to get the message out, but I didn't want to look like a fool. I made a split-second decision to go out there and perform without music.

I stepped onto the stage in the Atlanta auditorium and stood in front of thousands of people. Howie Mandel, Pierce Morgan, and Sharon Osborne greeted me, and I introduced myself as Metatron. I told them I was a personal injury lawyer in real life, but that Metatron was here to spread the message that humanity is evolving toward a higher state of consciousness. People in the crowd started booing before I even started the song. I started to realize that I was one of the gag acts. America's Got Talent chose me not because I was talented, but because I was funny and entertaining. I started the song:

I am Metatron. I am an angel of light. Here to light up the world and make everything alright.

By the time, I got out the first verse, half of the crowd was on their feet, booing. People with big X signs in their hands were jumping up and down, screaming, and the three judges buzzed me before I knew it. I stopped performing and stood there, embarrassed and humiliated, my mind spinning with thoughts of how foolish I had been. Howie Mandel asked me something, and I answered. I don't remember exactly what was said, but I was walking toward him as we were having a conversation, and I didn't realize that I had run out of real estate. I fell off the stage!

Fortunately, I landed on my feet. The only thing that hurt was my ego. Howie Mandel proceeded to make a joke at my expense. He said, "You came here to show us the light and the way, but you missed the lights at the end of the stage and you lost your way." It was actually really funny.

What had I done? I had embarrassed myself and my family. My law partners were going to be mortified. By that point, I had begun to seriously suspect that I might be delusional. Was I going through a mid-life crisis? Or was I just a guy who chose the wrong way to spread a positive message? I didn't realize it at the time, but things were about to get worse before they got better.

In May of 2011, the Metatron fail aired on national television, and it instantly became a massive hit on YouTube. People were ruthless in their criticism. Tallahassee, where I live and practice law, is a small city, and my face is plastered all over billboards and local television. Folks know who I am, especially in the legal community, and I lost credibility with a lot of people. People said I was delusional, and once again, I started to wonder if they were right—the only thing was, I still felt compelled to pursue my mission. Even public humiliation couldn't overpower my desire to do my part to make the world a better place. The lessons I learned have proven invaluable. I learned the importance of humility, I learned not to present myself as some kind of savior, and I learned that there's a difference between sharing my experience, with humility, and acting like a know-it-all.

One thing I asked myself after the Metatron debacle was, "Where was my higher self during all of this. Why didn't something inside of me tell me that I was on the wrong path?" I'm choosing to believe that my ego's desire to be the center of attention drowned out the voice of my higher self. At this point in my life, I'm grateful for the America's Got Talent experience. I still get embarrassed when I think about it, but the bigger the failure, the bigger the lesson. Whenever we reach the point where we can feel grateful for our failures, we know that we have reached a new level of effectiveness. We will be willing to take more risks, and thereby open ourselves up to greater rewards.

 Activity:

What do you need to release?

___

___

___

___

Who do you need to forgive?

___

___

_____
_____
_____

What in your life do you need to accept?

_____
_____
_____
_____
_____

Who or what thoughts do you need to release to become your higher self?

_____
_____
_____
_____
_____

Who do you need to become to achieve the goal you have set for yourself?

- Use this to identify your higher self – and love them!

_____
_____
_____
_____
_____

CHAPTER 17

IDENTIFY WHAT'S HOLDING YOU BACK

By now, you have set big, bold, amazing goals. You've set deadlines. You've created detailed scenarios that you visualize as your future. You've accepted that your past failures have taught you the lessons you needed to learn to put you on your highest path. The next step is to identify anything else inside of you, beyond fear, that might be holding you back. The main obstacle that holds people back from achieving their dreams is negative thinking, which includes but isn't limited to a fear of failure. All negative thought patterns serve as barriers to high achievement. Eliminate negative thought patterns, and you'll find yourself in a state of grace, where everything seems to magically fall into place.

The mind can only hold one thought at a time, be it positive or negative. By choosing to focus on the positive, you eliminate the negative, and you open up your mind to opportunities you never would have noticed had you continued focusing on the negative. A goal is a positive thought, which opens the mind to more positive thoughts that identify pathways to achieve the goal. The more often you think about your goal with the intent and expectation of achieving it, the clearer the path becomes, until at some point, the path becomes crystal-clear. Develop the discipline to follow the path, and the goal has no choice but to materialize.

Remember, you can't control everything that happens to you, but you can always control where you're headed. In every situation, regardless of how horrible it is or might seem, there is always an opportunity. If it doesn't kill you, it can make you stronger if you can develop the habit of extracting the positive from every situation.

What do you do when your house burns down?

"That's all great," you might say, "But how does positive thinking apply to real problems in real life?" Let me give you an example of what happened when my house burned down.

After my vision in 2011, I had some very prosperous years. My wife and I had always wanted to live in a particular neighborhood, one of the most prestigious neighborhoods in Tallahassee. The entrance road to the neighborhood has a canopy of trees that makes it look magical, especially one sunny days when the light sneaks through the leaves into the street. The first time I drove through that canopy, I thought it was the most beautiful neighborhood in the world. We were able to purchase a house there, and we put everything we had into renovating it. Our brand new furniture was light and airy, lots of white fabrics and white marble countertops, high-end everything. We planned on making it our forever home.

However, there was another house in the same neighborhood that caught our attention. It was clearly one of the most beautiful houses in the entire city, situated right at the end of the canopy road. It had been featured in two national magazines for its architecture and interior design. It was a lake-front Mediterranean style house with huge windows, a pool, three acres of land, massive oak trees in the yard, and a bridge to the lake. We passed by this house every time we went to our newly renovated home, and every time, we commented on how much we loved it. It was our dream house.

After we had finished the renovations on our new home, our dream house was put up for sale. We loved it so much, I called my best friend, who's a realtor, and asked him the selling price. He gave it to me, and I said, "I'll take it!" I told him to call the realtor who was listing it and lock down a deal immediately.

My friend called me back about twenty minutes later and said he'd made a mistake. He thought I was talking about another house for sale down the street. The dream house I wanted was listed for more than double what my friend had quoted me. Dang! I was disappointed, but we were still very happy with our newly renovated home.

About a week later, I was sitting at my desk at work when my receptionist came running into my office around 3:00 in the afternoon. She usually has a bubbly, cheery attitude, but this time she was deadly serious. "Jimmy, your house is on fire! You need to go." I jumped in my car and sped off. By the time I got there, smoke was coming out of every crevice of the house, and neighbors were gathered in my yard, watching the house burn. My wife was standing outside, holding my Maltese in her arms, crying. My neighbors were consoling her. Thank God everybody was fine. As I stood there, watching the house go up in smoke, I knew without a doubt in my mind that something good was going to come of this. I was concerned about my wife's and kids' feelings, but not once did I feel sad, angry, or upset about what was happening. I know this sounds weird, but by this time in my life, finding and focusing on the positive in every situation had become a deeply ingrained habit. I had completely surrendered to my highest self, and it was very hard for me to get upset about anything. Because I understood how good always arises out of bad, I was actually excited.

Fast forward to a couple of days later. I get a call from my realtor friend, who told me that the owners of the dream house had dropped their price by 20%. That was a huge drop, but I was still thinking it was out of my price range. Later that same day, I was having lunch with my wife, drinking a glass of wine as we talked about how to deal with the fallout of having lost our house and all our belongings. By pure chance, the interior designer of the dream house floated into the restaurant. We recognized her from the multi-page magazine article we saw featuring her showcasing our dream house.

"Hey, you're that famous designer, aren't you?" I said. "We saw you in the magazine and love what you did with the house in Rosehill."

We had never met this designer before, but she acted like she knew us her entire life. She looked like what you would expect from a high-end designer, rich and artsy, wearing Louis Vuitton boots, ripped jeans, and lots of chic jewelry. She just sat down at our table and said, "If you like the house, you should make an offer on it. I'm pretty close with the owners, and I'm sure they're not expecting to get what they're asking for it."

I knew at that moment we were meant to have the house. My wife and I made what we considered to be a low offer, and we started to negotiate. Long story short, we are living in our dream house right now and couldn't be happier. Not only did we purchase the house for less than we expected, but we also negotiated a deal that allowed us to keep the amazing furniture that was showcased in the interior design magazine! It was an added bonus and a necessity: all of our furniture got destroyed in the fire, and to this day, we are thankful to the owners.

When you develop the habit of seeking the positive in every situation, you never have a bad day. Everything "bad" that happens becomes an opportunity to create and attain something better. Any time you find yourself feeling a negative emotion, know that this emotion is the direct result of how and where you are choosing to focus your attention. Redirect your focus, and you change the emotion: if you want to feel good, focus on your master goal.

Let Go of Pain from the Past

One of my favorite lines from the movie Cocktail is, "Coughlin's law: Bury the dead; they stink up the joint." The past is gone. It's already history. Yet most people spend an unbelievable amount of time thinking about it. They think about their regrets. They think about the people who did them wrong. They replay old scenarios in their heads over and over, wondering what would have happened if the circumstances had been different. They hold onto grudges. They hold onto guilt. And the net result is that they are holding themselves back from achieving their dreams.

Remember the vision I had where I released the dark energy I had been storing in my subconscious mind? It was symbolic of me releasing pain from the past. If you recall, before that vision, I had a dream where the most evil person in my life told me, "I came to earth to play the role of an evil person so that you could learn the lessons you needed to learn to become the man you've become." It was through that dream that I was able to process the most important lesson in this book: the challenges we face in life are meant to teach us lessons so that we can become the highest version of ourselves. Through that dream, I was not only able to release the pain from my past, but I was also able to experience gratitude for the lessons that pain had taught me.

The most highly effective people are free from the baggage of their pasts. They don't feel the need to drudge up old pain, because they realize it serves no purpose. Energy flows where your attention goes. Think about the past, and you move backward. Think about the future—your mission and your master goal—and you move forward.

How to Release Pain from the Past

The irony is that in order the release the pain from the past, you must confront it. This is the inner work we all must do to become the highest version of ourselves. The first step is to identify the painful memory. Replay it in your mind. Allow yourself to feel the pain, the embarrassment, the anger as much as necessary so that the emotions attached to the memory dissipate. If you do this often enough, the emotion attached to it will fade, and you will soon begin to understand the positive role the experience played in teaching you the lessons you needed to learn. When a painful memory is liberated from the emotions that were attached to it, it becomes wisdom.

Journaling is one of the best ways to turn painful memories into wisdom. Writing an autobiography is another extremely powerful technique. Some people prefer psychotherapy. I like to meditate, which for me is basically sitting in silence. Jogging is great. Long walks in nature also present a perfect opportunity to confront your past. The important point is to set aside a certain amount of time every day with the goal of utilizing it to clear out the dark energy that's holding you back. You will eventually arrive at a state of gratitude and find yourself thankful for all of the challenges you faced in the past. When you reach that point, nothing can stop you from achieving your goals. Everything will seem as though it is magically falling into place. Some people call this living in the flow. I've heard others call it living in a state of grace.

The Hard Times We Suffer Add Depth and Meaning to the Good Times

Without a doubt, prison was the most painful experience of my life. It was also the most important experience I have ever had in terms of molding and shaping who I am today, because it forced me to see life from a different perspective. While I was waiting at the federal detention center, I remember looking out of the tiny window of my prison cell at the cars passing by on the roadway and thinking, "I wish I had the problems those people have."

The entire experience gave me a strength that I never would have had if I hadn't endured it. Now, when I'm having a bad moment, or a bad day, I think back on what I've been through and say to myself, "This isn't a bad day." When the judge put the hammer down and sentenced me to five years, that was a bad day. When an inmate threatened to rape me with a broomstick, that was a bad day. When another inmate came after me with a lock he'd balled up in his fist, that was a bad day. The problems I have now are a walk in the park.

If nothing else, the hard times we endure make us enjoy the good times even more. The hard times give us something to compare them to, thus adding depth and meaning to our enjoyment. These days, when I'm vacationing with my family on a tropical island in Hawaii, doing zip lines over a beautiful jungle or surfing in the crystal blue ocean, I feel an incredible amount of gratitude for this freedom. Or when I'm sitting in the back of my law firm's limo, drinking a bottle of good wine with my partners and toasting to our successes, in the back of my mind I'm thinking about how grateful I am to have come so far. If I had never gone to prison for two and a half years and experienced a complete lack of freedom, there is no way I would appreciate these experiences as much as I do. I'm thankful every day for having the opportunity to face these challenges, and overcome them.

 Activity:

1. Identify a painful memory.
2. Identify a lesson learned from that experience.
3. Write a sentence to thank that experience and the lesson you learned.

1. _____
   _____
2. _____
   _____
3. _____
   _____

CHAPTER 18

IDENTIFY NEGATIVE BELIEFS AND TURN THEM UPSIDE DOWN

Negative beliefs are one of the biggest reasons people fail. Beliefs are incredibly important— they dictate our perception of the world. We all see the world through a filter of beliefs, and we rarely have thoughts that are inconsistent with them. You are where you are today because of the beliefs you have held in your mind until now. Those beliefs created thoughts; those thoughts created emotions, which compelled you to take action. Those actions resulted in you moving in the direction of a particular future, the future that you find yourself experiencing right now. If you held different beliefs, you would have had different thoughts, felt different emotions, taken different actions, and stepped into an entirely different future.

The most important belief to examine is the belief you hold about who you are in relation to the rest of the universe. This is a core belief, out of which stems all of your other beliefs. If you believe you are just a tiny spec in a huge universe over which you have no control, you are destined for a chaotic and unfulfilling life. If you believe you are the master and creator of your own universe, you have a much better chance of experiencing the life you most desire. This makes sense, because if you believe you have no control over your life, you won't even bother trying to set goals. But if you believe you have total control, you will be a goal-setting machine, secure in the knowledge that you are destined to achieve what you dream.

Choose beliefs that make you feel powerful; discard all beliefs that make you feel inferior to your circumstances or inferior to someone else. Most people have never analyzed their beliefs to determine whether they are empowering or disempowering. The best way to identify a disempowering belief is to pay attention to how you feel. Whenever you feel down, depressed, sad, or negative, that feeling will always be tied to a disempowering belief. Usually, unhappy feelings are related to a feeling of being out of control. Decide now to believe that you are the master of your own destiny. The truth is that you always have been in total control, but perhaps you didn't realize it, and so you let go of the steering wheel. Your current circumstances are the result of your past beliefs, thoughts, actions, consequences. You may not be able to control your circumstances, because they are the result of decisions you have already made, but remember that you can always control where you are headed. Stay focused on your master goal, believe that it's your destiny to achieve the goal, move consistently in the direction of your goal, and you will succeed.

Watch Out for Conflicting Beliefs

Beliefs are like spokes in a wheel. Core beliefs are the hubs of the wheel. Most people have many core beliefs, each one of which has many beliefs that stem from it. But often people unknowingly harbor beliefs that conflict with one another, which is one sure way to block their energy flow. A common example I've heard is this: Jerry believes money is the root of all evil. Jerry also believes a bunch of money would make his life better. These beliefs cancel each other out, and as a result, Jerry's desire for money is unlikely to manifest itself into reality. It's much more likely that Jerry will stay poor for most of his life. His desire for money is being pulled back by his belief that money is the root of all evil.

The most powerful manifestors examine their own beliefs, discard those that hold them back, and power up those that work in their favor.

Choose Not to Believe in Luck

Most people believe that, to some degree, luck plays a role in whether somebody succeeds or fails. I've heard people say on many occasions, "I'd rather be lucky than good." This is an extremely disempowering belief. While it's true that people can benefit from luck in the short term, establishing luck as a long-term success plan is one of the easiest ways for people get distracted. Thinking about bad luck is a huge demotivator—and thinking about winning the lottery is a waste of time and energy that could be used to think about and pursue a master goal. Every time we think about our master goal, we are moving in the direction of achieving it. Every time we think about winning the lottery, we are wasting the opportunity to move in the direction of achieving our master goal. A master of self is careful with his or her thoughts, because every thought has a domino effect that leads to other thoughts, emotions, actions, and consequences.

 Activity:

    a) Write a negative belief based on the negative thoughts from previous chapter.
    b) For each belief identify if it is empowering or disempowering.

c) For each disempowering belief create a new empowering belief.
- Example: I'm not going to be good at that so why bother ⟶ I can do anything I put my mind to!

Belief #	Disempowering belief	New empowering belief

CHAPTER 19

UNITY CONSCIOUSNESS: THE ULTIMATE EMPOWERING BELIEF

The best way to eliminate negative beliefs is to develop a master belief that eradicates anything disempowering: a master belief that powers you up. Through the experiences I've described in this book, I developed a belief in what I call unity consciousness. Unity consciousness trumps all disempowering beliefs because it acknowledges that we are all connected, we are all different parts of the same collective consciousness, and that everything I do affects you, and everything you do affects me. As a result, every single one of us not only has the power to change the entire world, we do so with every thought we have, every decision we make. This is a big deal.

Like every species that has evolved before us, humanity has two possible destinations: we can either continue to adapt and evolve, or we can allow ourselves to eventually become extinct. The idea of "evolve to thrive" applies to every organized system—every business, every community, every species, and even every human being. Change is inevitable, and we must all adapt. But the question arises, "What are we evolving toward?" If we are going to thrive and maximize our experience as human beings, what is the ultimate goal? I am postulating the idea that humanity is evolving toward unity consciousness, the conscious awareness that we are all connected to everyone else and everything else. More than that, I am making the case that unity consciousness is the master key to success in every endeavor, from building a business to nourishing a relationship to winning a baseball game. Unity consciousness is the ultimate empowering belief.

What is Unity Consciousness?

The idea of unity consciousness has become somewhat cliché and is often misunderstood. A popular joke is, "What did the Dali Lama say when he walked into the pizza shop? Make me one with everything." Coaches and athletes are sometimes heard saying, "Be the ball," but often neither the coach nor the athlete knows what it means to become one with an apparently inanimate object. People seem to understand on some level that there is power behind the idea of unity consciousness, but most people never stop to think about what being one with everything really means in a practical sense.

Unity consciousness is the belief that we are one with each other as well as the rest of creation. It is the result of knowing that everything in existence is part of an intricate whole. Everything is connected. This connection is so intimate that even a relatively minor event in the universe, such as a single thought, affects all of existence for all of eternity. Think back to the discussion about the Butterfly Effect. Tiny changes in conditions change the entire equation that makes up our reality.

Unlike many sentient beings, human beings are self-aware and enjoy apparent freedom of thought. A person with unity consciousness knows that every thought, every decision, and every action they take is a monumental act of creation whose ripple effects extend out into eternity; that it places every human being in a position of unlimited power. The net result is that not only do humans have the ability and drive to utilize that power, but they also have a sense of responsibility to all of existence and a deep desire to contribute to the positive evolution of humanity.

Every person in the world is caught up in an evolutionary wave. Some people resist the wave and get pummeled. They are swimming into the wave instead of flowing with it. Those who catch the wave can enjoy ride of their lives. The good news is this: Because every person is an intricate part of the whole, the system is rigged so that anybody who wants to catch the wave can ride it. It's rigged, because we are all in this together, all for one and one for all. The reality we experience is the result of a collective consciousness, where the evolution of one of us uplifts the entire global community. Collectively, we have the opportunity to shift to a world where people understand their true power as co-creators of reality. We are shifting away from separation consciousness, which has plagued our society for all of recorded history.

Separation consciousness is the belief in the illusion that we are separate from each other and from the whole of creation—as opposed to individualized parts of a single unified consciousness—and it results in a dangerous conviction that nothing we do really matters. We all suffer from separation consciousness to one degree or another. A person with severe separation consciousness feels isolated and alone in a big, uncaring world, disconnected from the rest of humanity and everything else. Separation consciousness can lead to horrible, criminal behavior. Every murder, rape, robbery, or violent act of any kind arises in part because the victimizer feels disconnected from the victim to some extent.

On the other hand, a person with unity consciousness feels a sense of family, safety, and inner peace. They follow the golden rule of the New Testament, "Love thy neighbor as thyself." They feel deeply, intimately connected to the rest of humanity and the universe as a whole, and they know that they matter. Unity consciousness is the cause of all good in the world. Acts of kindness and love arise from a feeling of connection.

A person with unity consciousness is in flow with the universe and experiences a life of synchronicities and pleasant surprises. They can manifest desires easily and effortlessly because their desires are in alignment with the collective desire to evolve in a positive way.

Imagine a world where every human being feels a deep connection to every other human being, the planet, and all of creation. Imagine if everybody knew beyond the shadow of a doubt that everything we do, every thought we have, every emotion we feel, and every action we take affects every other person on the planet and the entire whole of creation. Imagine a world where everybody accepts their true power as co-creators of reality and utilizes that power responsibly. We could build a paradise on earth.

I believe humanity is headed in that direction. Deep down, we all want a world where people feel safe, loved, protected, and connected—a world where people honor each other's innate talents and power to change the world; a world where hunger no longer exists because people take care of each other; where people no longer fear each other; where people support each other and cooperate to continually make the world a better place for everyone. We want a world where work is fun and fulfilling, where people automatically welcome and accept even the strangest of strangers, and where the overarching energy is love. The possibilities of what we can create, the technologies that can be used if we work together in the spirit of cooperation, are beyond anything we can currently imagine.

In Unity Consciousness, We all Grow Together

In unity consciousness, we are constantly evolving toward a better, more self-aware society. Think about how well we live today compared to people in times past. We can go to the grocery story any day and purchase any kind of food we desire. People used to have to hunt for their food. Today, we can go to restaurants at any time and eat amazing cuisine from all around the world. The quality of the food, and the amazing recipes we know today, have also evolved. Many of the people alive today, including me, live better, easier, more comfortable, and more abundant lives than kings and queens lived centuries ago. We can communicate with people across the globe immediately with our cell phones. People used to have to communicate long distance by mail that was delivered via foot couriers, or not at all. We can fly all over the world in airplanes. People used to have to travel by foot or on horses. Healthcare has evolved. Entertainment has evolved. Our language has evolved. The internet has brought us all closer together. Social media is keeping people more closely connected. The world is improving in a million ways.

Some people might disagree with the above paragraph, but I would suggest that those people look at the numbers. I saw a Ted's Talk recently that revealed some interesting numbers: compared to just thirty years ago, people are living longer, crime is down, homicide is down, wars are less prevalent, poverty is way down globally, and democracy is on the rise. Two hundred years ago, 90% of the world's population persisted in severe poverty. Today, less than 10%. This could be the topic of an entirely different book, but suffice it to say, life is getting better for humanity as a collective whole. Imagine how challenging life would have been a few hundred years ago, before we had all of the modern conveniences that we enjoy today.

In Unity Consciousness, You Are the Center of the Universe

Human life is an experience of conscious awareness. To each of us, there appears to be one reality, the reality we can see, smell, taste, touch, and hear. We become aware of the information that floods our senses—light photons, sound vibrations, etc.—and we call this reality. However, consciousness is not limited to this one reality. Dreams are a perfect of example of experiences in consciousness that exist on an entirely different plane. There are literally an infinite number of possible realities, and the human life experience is simply the experience of one such possibility. More than that, it is the experience of but one possible timeline within the parameters of one possible reality system. On this planet, there are currently more than seven billion people, each experiencing their own realities within the parameters of the reality program we call Earth.

Our consciousness is the center of everything. We have all been given the power of free will, the power to direct our conscious awareness. Our consciousness is swimming in a sea of infinite possibilities, and is in fact the center of everything from our perspective. As if we were swimming in a boundless ocean, every time we move, the entire universe shifts to accommodate us.

Most of us have been brought up thinking it's wrong to believe that we are the center of the universe. We've all heard, "You think the world revolves around you?" at some point in our lives.

But in unity consciousness, being the center of everything means the exact opposite of being selfish. It means embracing the reality that everything we do matters to the rest of the world. In actuality, the universe waits with bated breath for our next thought to arise, for our next decision, for our next action, because whatever choice me make will determine the direction of our collective reality. The rest of the world is counting on each and every one of us. For this reason, being in unity consciousness carries with it not only a tremendous amount of power, but also a tremendous amount of responsibility.

For these reasons, unity consciousness represents the ultimate empowering belief system. I realize these claims might sound grandiose, but the failure of human beings to recognize their true power has plagued this world forever. People who don't recognize their true power are careless with their thoughts and actions. But people in a state of unity consciousness know, beyond a doubt, that what they do matters, and they act responsibly as a result.

We Are All Living in Our Own World

Each of us is experiencing an entirely unique reality. This has been proven over and over again through studies related to human perception, where one person sees an image and interprets it one way, while another person sees the same image and interprets it in an entirely different manner. As a trial lawyer, I can present the exact same case with the exact same evidence to six people sitting in a jury box, and every one of them will see the case in a completely different way.

Studies have shown that the human brain has a dual function of taking in information from the environment and interpreting that information through a lens of perception. The information taken from the environment gets filtered by the brain in a way that excludes anything inconsistent with the individual's belief system. With the limited information that gets through the filter, the brain then fills in the gaps by creating fluid images, sounds, and sensory experiences consistent with the experiencer's expectations. These expectations are formulated through past conditioning and can be altered by the experiencer's conscious choice to change their expectations. In this sense, the idea that we live in a world of our own making is true, but it is more accurate to say that we choose to perceive the information that is available to us in a certain way. Our physical senses are detecting data—light, sound, vibration, matter—and how we interpret that data becomes our reality. We are not creating our reality, but our perception is navigating us through a field of potentials. When we direct our focus, we activate a single potential consistent with our expectations.

Since a single event can be interpreted in an infinite number of ways, how we choose to interpret the events of our lives determines the reality we live in. This is powerful. Most people never make a conscious choice to change their perception, but that's only because most people have no idea of their true power. Nevertheless, if we want to skillfully navigate infinite potential futures, we must start by changing our expectations, and thereby changing our perception of the world around us. Here's the exciting part. By changing our core beliefs, we change our perception, and as a result, the world around us changes to match our expectations. We tune into a different channel on the cosmic television, which contains every program you can imagine. Remember the Mercedes story at the beginning of the book and how the Mercedes manifested in my life, despite me not even trying. I believe that when I repeatedly wrote down the goal of owning the Mercedes while in prison, I tuned into a bunch of possible future realities, all of which included me getting the Mercedes in some way shape or form. By repeating the goal with so much emotion and passion,

I closed off all possible futures where the Mercedes did not manifest in my life. So, the art of navigating multiple possible futures is not just about changing our perception to see the world through rose-colored lenses. Changing our perception actually results in tuning into a different future reality. It results in a change in our thoughts, emotions, and actions, which results in our experience of the physical manifestation of a reality consistent with our new perception. If we are poor, we can become rich. If we are angry, we can become happy.

Everything Works Together for Good

In unity consciousness, there are no accidents. There are only potentials. You, being the consciousness navigating through the sea of potentials, have the power to navigate into choppy waters, or into calm seas with blue skies and sunshine. Every time you navigate into choppy waters, you have the opportunity to learn and improve your navigational skills. If you are paying attention, you will soon discover what you do not want. You will learn what not to do moving forward. And as a result, you will ultimately become a skilled navigator. The reality program we call Earth is very much about learning to navigate our conscious awareness.

This belief has served me in too many ways to count. Every time something happens that appears to be a setback, I immediately search for the hidden opportunity. I automatically know that the apparent set back is simply a sign that I need to shift directions, try a different tact, or that something better is available that I'd previously missed—like when my house burned down. I immediately knew something good would come of it, and I ended up in my absolute dream house.

 Activity:

How differently would you live your life if you believed your actions directly affected all humanity and creation?

_____
_____
_____
_____
_____

Which of your perceptions have changed since starting this book/program?

_____
_____
_____
_____
_____

CHAPTER 20

LIVING IN THE FLOW

There have been numerous books, videos, and seminars about the idea of living in the flow, or living in a state of grace. There is a state of consciousness where everything seems to fall into place, and it feels as though life is creating a beautiful path just for you. Manifesting your desires is easy and fun. When you are living in the flow or a state of grace, nothing can get you down.

The idea of living in the flow sounds like fairy magic, so I want to take a moment to dispel that notion. There is logic behind it. Painful emotions hold us back, because they create fear. We don't want to experience the pain again, so we're afraid to try new things. We're afraid to set big, bold, audacious goals out of a fear of failure, a fear of embarrassment, or a fear of criticism. Not only that, but painful memories also create self-doubt, which reduces our motivation to pursue our dreams.

However, when the painful memory loses the emotions that are attached to it and transforms itself into wisdom, we suddenly have the courage to try new things. We know that every failure carries with it the lessons we need to learn to try again, this time with more information, or to shift directions toward something even better. We stop letting fear hold us back. We stop having painful flashbacks that distract us from our goals. As a result, we are able to direct our attention toward our master goal and keep it there.

Harnessing the Power of Concentration

To successfully navigate the sea of infinite possibilities, keep your mind focused on your master goal. The more often we can stay focused on our master goal, the more likely it is that the goal will come to fruition. Whenever we find ourselves thinking about the past, thinking about our fears, or wasting time thinking about things that do little for us—social media, television, obsessively checking the news—we should gently pull our concentration back to our master goal.

Practice this every day. You will eventually develop the habit of always thinking about your master goal. When thinking about your master goal becomes your default setting, nothing will be able to stop you. Your subconscious mind has no choice but to lead you into a future where your goal comes to fruition.

Every morning, I wake up thinking about my mission in life and my master goal, and I go to bed thinking about it every night. I think about it all day, and it drives my actions day in and day out. Don't get me wrong, I take time to enjoy my family and spend time with my wife, and when I'm with them, I am intent on giving them my full attention. But I am absolutely obsessed with pursuing my mission and reaching my master goal. My mission is my hobby. My master goal is how I measure my effectiveness in pursuing my mission. It's what I do for fun other than spending time with the people I love. I'm getting pumped up right now just thinking about it.

 Activity:

Other than your Big Master Goal, identify your top 3 priorities

- Ex. time for family, god, self love – find balance

1. _____

2. _____

3. _____

How did you decide on these priorities?

_____
_____
_____
_____
_____

CHAPTER 21

SOME FINAL THOUGHTS

The message of this book can be summarized like this: You matter. Everything you do matters. Every thought you have matters. Every action you take matters. The way you respond to your most difficult challenges matters. You have the power to change this world. In fact, you are changing the world every moment of every day. Now is the moment to claim your power and start changing the world in a conscious way. Decide your mission, and pursue it with all of your being. Create a master goal to measure your progress. Write down your goals and make plans to accomplish them. Endeavor to make this world a better place. We are all counting on you.